THE HOMICIDAL, OBSESSIVE, AND DELUSIONAL WOMEN OF THE BIBLE – OLD TESTAMENT

The Mess and Messages of Their Lives

BY – JACQUELINE ROGERS

Contents

Dedication

This book is lovingly dedicated to the memory of my mother, Ida Bell Rogers. She walked a rough road to make it a little bit smoother for me. She sacrificed much to make sure that I could have opportunities she didn't. She was a quiet, caring person, and the lessons she taught me were more in deed than in word. So I always thank God for her life and the time we had together. She was the best mother I could have possibly had. Until I see her again, I will always appreciate how hard she worked each and every day of her life to send me out into the world <u>always</u> with a belly full, happy, shiny, and new.

Introduction

I chose to write about three women of the Old Testament Leah, Michal, and Athaliah—because each of these women had so much going for themselves and so much to live for. But each by their own hands managed to destroy themselves and others as well. I saw so much of myself in them.

Why did Leah constantly put herself forth to be a victim—a martyr for madness, used and abused, disrespected and neglected? Why did Michal hold on to a fantasy and deliberately refuse to grasp reality? Why was Athaliah so insecure, and why did she mask it so violently?

In seeking the answers to these questions; examining their lives and their disturbing proclivities, it forced me to face my own. I am no stranger to some of their sins.

I wrote this book as I continue to work out my salvation (Philippians 2:12-13). I wrote this book as I grow in knowledge and wisdom. I wrote this book as a cautionary note to myself that I now share with you.

All praise to my Lord and Savior Jesus Christ!

Jacqueline Rogers

Michal

THE MAN OF HER DREAMS

Michal

Jeremiah 48:29-30 – "…her overweening pride and conceit, her pride and arrogance and the haughtiness of her heart. I know her insolence but it is futile," declares the Lord, "and her boasts accomplish nothing."

We first meet Michal in 1 Samuel 14:49. Her name means "who is like God." She was the youngest child of Saul meaning "asked," a tall, handsome man born into wealth and privilege (1 Samuel 9:1-2). He was chosen by God at the behest of the people to be Israel's first king (1 Samuel 8:4-5, 12:12-13).

Michal's mother was Ahinoam, meaning "my brother is joy." No doubt, she was a beautiful woman. Can you imagine the aristocratic Kish (Saul's father) arranging for anything less for his son?[1] Michal's grandfather on her mother's side was Ahimaaz, whose name means "powerful brother" (1 Samuel 14:50). He was probably a man of like influence and social standing as was Saul's father, Kish. That Michal came from such a family of powerful and influential men had quite an impact on her character, as the coming years would show. The structure of Biblical society, particularly during the Old Testament period, was patriarchal—the rule of the father. And according to this rule, the duties of the father from king on down were to provide and protect and most importantly be the spiritual head of the family, providing the moral compass from which the family took their direction.

---

1 According to the custom of the day, parents with the father playing the lead role selected wives for their sons based on the young woman's ability to fit into the family/clan and her hoped-for ability to have children (sons) for her husband to increase and strengthen that family/clan.

Saul really never lived up to these responsibilities. He was a reluctant warrior, more at war with himself than against the Philistines.[2] His family pedigree and good looks weren't enough to fend off the personal demons that eventually destroyed him and his entire family.

He would cause the death of his sons: Jonathan, Abinadab, and Malki-Shua (Samuel 31:1–3). He would constantly use his daughters—Merab, (increase) and Michal—for his own political gain. Nevertheless Saul was their father and the king, and they stood by him until the end.

Especially in the eyes of his youngest, Michal, Saul would always be a hero. In her eyes, Saul would always be that valiant warrior she heard so much about while growing up. Her favorite story was when her father fought against the ruthless Nahash of the Ammonites (1 Samuel 11:1–11) and saved the people of Jabesh Gilead. She never tired of hearing it, and she always saw her father that way, a heroic man who saved the day. In Michal's eyes, Saul could do no wrong.

Perhaps because of the appeal and longing for heroic feats, Michal found herself drawn to a teenage boy only a little older than she.

---

2 Ancient enemies of Israel, who originated from Caphtor (*Genesis 10:14*). It was partly because of their aggression that Israel requested a king (*1Samuel 8:19-20*). Saul was at war against the Philistines during his entire reign (*1Samuel 14:52*).

Hero Worship

Soon we'll be married and raise a family.
A cozy, little home out in the country with two children maybe three.
I tell you, I can visualize it all.
This couldn't be a dream for too real it all seems…
But it was just my imagination, running away with me.
It was just my imagination running away with me…

—Just My Imagination (Running Away with Me), The Temptations©

The lyrics to that popular song by The Temptations give an apt description of Michal's relationship with David. Ostensibly, it is the old story of a boy from the wrong side of the tracks who gets the girl. In this case, it's the shepherd boy who gets the princess. Theirs was that fine romance based more on fantasy (Michal's) than fact, and the harder Michal worked the fantasy, the more she kept bumping her head against the fact that there are some things, and there are some people, that are never meant to be.

1 Samuel 17:57-58 – As soon as David returned from killing the Philistine, Abner took him and brought him before Saul, with David still holding the Philistine's head. "Whose son are you young man?" Saul asked him. David said, "I am the son of your servant Jesse of Bethlehem."

Michal may have first become aware of David after he returned from that Philistine campaign where he killed the soldier of fortune, Goliath. She may have caught a glimpse of him speaking with her oldest brother, Jonathan. Maybe one day she followed the sound of a harp and saw David playing before her father. Michal had heard he was a skilled fighter, perhaps Israel's best, young as he was. She wouldn't have thought someone so fierce on the battlefield would be so skillful a musician as well…especially on the harp[3] (1Samuel 16:14-18).

There were so many things Michal wondered about this young man who seemed to come out of nowhere. She noticed that Jonathan had befriended David and spoke well of him (1 Samuel 18:1- 4, 19:1). But Michal also noticed that just the mention of David's name had begun to make her father uneasy. She sensed a tenseness about him that had not been there before that Philistine battle (1 Samuel 18:6 -12). Truth be known, David made Michal uneasy as well. She heard the women sing his praises (1Samuel 18:6 -7). Now the more she thought about him, the more she saw him, Michal began to understand why. Here was a courageous warrior as well as a passionate musician and poet.[4] David was unlike any hero Michal had ever imagined.

1 Samuel 18:20 – Now Saul's daughter Michal was in love with David.

Michal was a young girl, probably in her early to mid-teens (Biblical scholars put her age around 14). David was thought to have been only a few years older. Both were of age to marry.[5] However, David was neither from her class nor her tribe, he being a shepherd from Bethlehem of the tribe Judah and she of royalty from the tribe of Benjamin.[6] But the more Michal saw him, the more she heard about him, none of that mattered…initially.

---

3 The harp is mentioned in the Bible more often than any other musical instrument. It was considered an aristocratic instrument usually made of ivory or silver. It was played for both sacred ceremonies and secular occasions.

4 Described as "the sweet psalmist of Israel" (*2 Samuel 23:1*) KJV. Out of 150 Psalms, almost half (73) are ascribed as "of David." David's expression of his relationship with God is unparalleled in its depth and range of emotions.

5 During the times of the Old Testament, there were no restrictions on the age when persons could marry, and often the betrothal occurred when they were pre-teens. By the time of the New Testament, the minimum age for marriage was set at 13 for boys and 12 for girls.

6 According to the Mosaic Law, marriage was preferred between two people of the same tribe (*Numbers 36:5-9*).

Just as Michal was experiencing young love, her father was in the throes of a mid-life crisis with the requisite feelings of loss and doubt. During this time, Saul was approximately midpoint in his 42-year reign as king of Israel (1 Samuel 13:1).[7] He had gone from a man anointed by God to one rejected by God because of his lack of humility and sense of entitlement that made it hard for him to acknowledge and accept the consequences of his disobedience against God's Word (1 Samuel 13: 7-14, 15:1-30). Years had passed since he and Jonathan had devised military campaigns. The memory of his heroics at Jabesh Gilead was just that. After Jabesh Gilead, there would be no more military victories for Saul.[8]

However, the most acute sense of loss and doubt Saul felt, which heightened his animosity toward David, was Jonathan's loss of confidence in him as a military leader as well as king.

1 Samuel 18:3-4 – And Jonathan made a covenant with David because he loved him as himself. Jonathan took off the robe he was wearing and gave it to David, along with his tunic and even his sword, his bow and his belt.[9]

It had been a long time coming. Over the years, Jonathan, a skillful warrior himself (1 Samuel 14:1-14), had seen the disastrous impact of his father's leadership on the military (1 Samuel 14:24-30, 17:11) and the nation

---

7 Saul was 30 years old when he became king. By the time of David, Saul was in his mid to late 40s.

8 During his reign, Saul also fought against Moab, the Ammonites, Edom, the kings of Zobah (an Aramean kingdom northeast of Damascus) in addition to the Philistines. *1 Samuel 14:47-48* says "*he inflicted punishment on them.*" But Saul did not defeat them as David did (*2 Samuel 8*).

9 Jonathan divests himself of entitlement (*1 Samuel 20:30-34*) and recognizes David as God's not Saul's heir apparent to sit on the throne of Israel. The robe/mantle symbolized favor and honor (*Genesis 37:3, 41:42*). The tunic that was worn under the robe denotes David's closeness to God in contrast to Saul's estrangement. The sword, bow, and belt symbolized David and his descendants (culminating in Jesus Christ) as the one to defeat Israel's enemies by the power of the Holy Spirit and the truth of God's Holy Word (*Ephesians 6:17*).

(1 Samuel 15:1). Jonathan loved his father but he loved Israel as well. That last battle against the Philistines made it crystal clear. His father couldn't inspire the army to win because of his loss of courage (1Samuel 17:2-11). Saul was so full of fear and dread he doubted himself and everyone else including God (1Samuel 17:21-24, 32-38). It brought Jonathan to the painful conclusion that his father was not the man to lead Israel to victory over its enemies.

Not only Jonathan, but Saul's own army and the people were becoming more inclined toward David (1 Samuel 18:5, 13-16). With the killing of Goliath as well as subsequent victories over the Philistines, David was garnering top billing as the hero for the times. Saul, who had personally recruited David primarily for entertainment purposes (1 Samuel 16:14-23), now watched helplessly from the sidelines as the understudy took center stage.

1 Samuel 18:6-8 – When the men were returning home after David had killed the Philistine, the women came out from all the towns of Israel to meet King Saul with singing and dancing, with joyful songs and with tambourines and lutes. As they danced they sang: "Saul has slain his thousands and David his tens of thousands." Saul was very angry; this refrain galled him.

The extent to which Saul feared David as a threat is not seen by Michal at first. While Jonathan knew and sensed God's anointing on David, it's never written that Michal did. If she did, it is unlikely that she cared. It mattered little to Michal that God chose David to be king over Israel. What mattered to Michal is that *she* chose David. It was never about David's anointing but the action—the heroic acts like her father used to do that drew Michal to him.

Girls quite often take after their fathers and frequently look for their fathers in any male with whom they choose to have a relationship with. That's what Michal saw in David—a larger-than-life person like her father who could satisfy her need for drama.

In reading the David and Michal narrative, it's apparent that Michal didn't love David but instead loved the *idea* of David, or better yet, she had a tremendous crush on him, not unusual for a girl her age. But as time moved on, Michal's feeling never really developed beyond this.

As Michal's household was becoming more stressful due to the issues of her father, the idea of a "David" could not have come at a better time. With storm clouds brewing from within and without her father's kingdom, here was someone Michal could ride off into the sunset with. Here was her happily ever after, just as she imagined it should be.

Proverbs 16:21 – The wise in heart are called discerning....

However, as much as Michal professed her love for David, nothing in God's Holy Word, in any version, speaks of David's love for her. In fact, Scripture doesn't even record a conversation between them until the documented end of their relationship (2 Samuel 6:20-22). As beautiful and refined as Michal probably was, David never loved her. Michal didn't notice this...at first. So "in crush" was she with David that she willfully ignored the complete absence of emotions on his part toward her. It was all about how David made her feel that was the driving force of their relationship.

Whereas true love gets its energy from the give and take between two people, a crush derives all its energy from the self-created fantasy of one. With eyes wide open, Michal didn't see that she was trying to be in a relationship with a person who had no emotional stake in it.

Unholy Matrimony

When Saul found out about his daughter's feelings for David, he sought to use them to circumvent God's rejection of him as king (1 Samuel 15:23-29). So what if it meant manipulating his youngest daughter, his baby girl? Both of them would get what they wanted. Michal would get David, and Saul would get David out of the way. The end would justify the means. And Saul meant to stay on the throne.

1 Samuel 18:20–21 – Now Saul's daughter Michal was in love with David, and when they told Saul about it, he was pleased. "I will give her to him," he thought, "so that she may be a snare to him and so that the hand of the Philistines may be against him." So Saul said to David, "Now you have a second opportunity to become my son-in-law."

Saul had initially promised the hand of Merab, his oldest daughter, to any man who killed Goliath (1 Samuel 17:25). He used David's sense of honor to renege on this promise (1 Samuel 18:17–19). But David's growing popularity sent Saul's paranoia into overdrive and required him to now use a different tactic. The mirror on the wall no longer gave Saul the answer he wanted to hear, but instead what he already knew—he was no longer the fairest of them all.

In Biblical times, when a woman was chosen as a wife, a bride price was paid by the groom to the father of the bride.[10] However, it should be said that Michal was never chosen. Jesse, David's father, did not choose Michal. David did not choose Michal. Rather Michal was recruited by her father quite willingly by the way, but recruited none-the-less, and none-the-less a price had to be paid.

---

10 The bride price was an agreed-upon payment between the parents of the betrothed. It could either be in money or services that were given to the father of the bride as compensation for the loss of a daughter and the work she provided for the family, as well as the loss of subsequent offspring.

1 Samuel 18:22–25 – Then Saul ordered his attendants: "Speak to David privately and say, 'Look the king is pleased with you, and his attendants all like you; now become his son-in-law.'" They repeated these words to David. But David said, "Do you think it's a small matter to become the king's son-in-law? I'm only a poor man and little known." When Saul's servants told him what David had said, Saul replied, "Say to David, 'The king wants no other price for the bride than a hundred Philistine foreskins to take revenge on his enemies.'" Saul's plan was to have David fall by the hands of the Philistines.[11]

Proverbs 26:27 – If a man digs a pit, he will fall into it; if a man rolls a stone, it will roll back on him.

Now the bride price Saul devised wasn't so much a price but a test, one that Saul desperately wanted David to fail (1 Samuel 18:24-25). To Saul's dismay, but by God's design, David passed the test with flying colors, delivering not one but 200 Philistine foreskins to Saul (1 Samuel 18:26-27). By this act, David unwittingly foretold and confirmed the futures of both Saul and Michal. Spiritually, the number two denotes difference or confirmation, either of good or evil. From this point on, the contrast between Saul and David would grow starker. Saul would be forever sending David to battles he himself could no longer fight. David would show himself to be twice the man that Saul was. It would become clearer and clearer that the Lord was no longer with Saul, that he had severed all ties.

For Michal, this bloody betrothal would foretell the fate of her father and brothers. It would also portend Michal being cut off from her privileged status as Saul's daughter and as David's wife. Ultimately it foretold her future in the Kingdom of Israel regarding children.

1 Samuel 18:27 – Then Saul gave him his daughter Michal in marriage.

---

11   David would employ a similar tactic, this time successfully with Uriah the Hittite in regards to his relationship with Bathsheba – *2 Samuel 11:14-15 – In the morning David wrote a letter to Joab and sent it with Uriah. In it he wrote, "Put Uriah in the front line where the fighting is fiercest. Then withdraw from him so he will be struck down and die."*

In Biblical times, wedding celebrations usually lasted a week. But when David and Michal married, God's Word doesn't speak of any such event taking place. They were a celebrity couple: a princess and a war hero, hmm…. Neither is there mention of the marriage being consummated. We assume that it was.[12] However, there are no phrases of love and lust, such as described in David's relationship with Bathsheba.

2 Samuel 11:4 – Then David sent some messengers to get her. She came to him, and he slept with her.

2 Samuel 12:24 – Then David comforted his wife Bathsheba, and he went to her and lay with her.

Many things that define true love or even passion are totally absent from the David and Michal narrative, beginning with the wedding. For that brief and shining moment, Michal and David were that "cutest couple." But time would tell it to be a relationship where there was no cause for celebration.

However party or not, Michal had her David. She had a *husband – A HUSBAND! And a HERO!*

> *Gee, I really love you and we're gonna get married,*
> *goin' to the chapel of love.*
> *Bells will ring, the sun will shine (whoa-whoa-whoa).*
> *I'll be his and he'll be mine.*
> *We'll love until the end of time.*

---

12 Once the marriage took place, the custom was for the couple to go to the groom's house, where they would be escorted to the bridal chamber. Guests would wait to hear the announcement that the couple had consummated their marriage (and that the bride's virginity was confirmed). Once that had been done, the festivities continued.

And we'll never be lonely anymore
because we're goin' to the chapel and we're gonna get married....

—The Chapel of Love, The Dixie Cups©

A Window of Opportunity

1 Samuel 18:30 – The Philistine commanders continued to go out to battle, and as often as they did, David met with more success than the rest of Saul's officers, and his name became well known.

After the marriage and honeymoon, David's popularity continued to grow. To Saul's dismay, marriage to Michal didn't slow David down one bit. Saul concluded that the only way to stop David was to kill him, and he would no longer be subtle about it. Saul no longer used the pretense of a military campaign against the Philistines to trap David. In fact, Saul and his army would begin to pursue David with just as much intensity, if not more, than toward the Philistines. From then on, Saul would spend the rest of his life in the futility of trying to kill David, which was a roundabout way of trying to destroy the plans of God.

Psalm 21:11 – Though they plot evil against you and devise wicked schemes, they cannot succeed…

Knowing the depth of friendship between his son and David, in desperation, Saul tried to enlist Jonathan and the household attendants to prove their love and loyalty to him by killing David. They respectively declined (1 Samuel 19:1).

Saul's frustration and desperation must have made the tension in the household unbearable due to his emotional outbursts, which were becoming more and more frequent (1 Samuel 18:10-11, 19:9-10). And with each outburst, Michal may have sensed that the time was growing short, when even Jonathan could reason with her father in regards to David (1 Samuel 19:4-5). After Saul's second attempt to kill David himself Michal finally warned David to run for his life.

1 Samuel 19:11–14 – Saul sent men to David's house to watch it and to kill him in the morning. But Michal, David's wife, warned him, "If you don't run for your life tonight, tomorrow you'll be killed." So Michal let David down through a window, and he fled and escaped. Then Michal took an idol and laid it on the bed, covering it with a garment and putting some goat's hair on the head. When Saul sent the men to capture David, Michal said, "He is ill."

This was the first of only three times Michal is referred to as David's wife as she helps him escape from her father. Interestingly, Michal is left with what she has loved all along…an idol.

Ezekiel 20:16 –…for their hearts were devoted to their idols.

As the youngest daughter of a rich, indulgent father, it's not surprising that Michal had idols. After all, she idolized Saul. But it is surprising she had an idol in the bedroom she shared with her husband. For Michal, David was, and would always be, that "someday my prince would come." Even after the ceremony, Michal held on to an idolized version of what a marriage and her husband should be like. The goat hair symbolized Michal's stubborn refusal to be in relationship with David the man, choosing instead the idea of David she had fashioned in her head and heart. She married a man, but it was an idol she longed to be intimate with. At the time, Michal didn't know that by holding onto an idol, a real man, whereby she could have experienced real love, was passing her by or better yet escaping out of a window.

David probably jumped for joy out of that window—out of Michal's life. David was always deliriously happy in two places: on the battlefield or in worship. In Gibeah (the capital of Saul's kingdom), he probably felt restless, pressed into the role of a trophy husband. For Michal, David was her knight in shining armor, no dents allowed. But David was a man in every sense of the word— warts and all. David was a man with needs outside the role of being her husband that Michal never considered, understood, or even cared about.

Looking at the relationships David had with other women, we see how different they are compared to his relationship (or lack thereof) with Michal. For Michal, David was her superhero. Abigail however, saw David as a real man instead of a fairy-tale character (1 Samuel 25:1–42). [13] She saw David as a man who could be vengeful, but she also saw him as God's man and a great friend. Bathsheba would see David as a man full of passion, capable of adultery, manipulation, and murder. But she would also know him as God's man, full of repentance, compassion, and devotion (2 Samuel 11, Psalm 51).

Abigail and Bathsheba both had the spiritual awareness and maturity to look beyond David's flaws. They brought out the best in him. They spoke to his anointing. With Michal, the only thing that would matter was David's relationship with her, nothing else. She claimed to love David but had no interest in what he loved best—his relationship with God.

---

13 Abigail, meaning "father of joy," was the wife of an abusive man named Nabal. David, while running from Saul, had asked Nabal for food for him and his men. Nabal refused. Abigail, acting in wisdom, provided food for them instead. By her actions she saved Nabal from David's revenge and David from carrying it out thus dishonoring his anointing. David subsequently married her (*1 Samuel 25: 1-42*).

Time Will Tell

After helping David escape, Michal revealed just how much she had learned from her father in terms of manipulation and deceit.

1 Samuel 19:17 – Saul said to Michal, "Why did you deceive me like this and send my enemy away so that he escaped?" Michal told him, "He said to me, Let me get away. Why should I kill you?"

Michal used her father's hatred of David to manipulate him and maintain her position in his household and in his heart at the same time. The Bible doesn't say whether Michal asked to go with David. All we know is, in the end, she stayed with her father and the idols.

Jonah 2:8 – Those who cling to worthless idols forfeit the grace that could be theirs.

Michal was left alone for what she thought would only be a short time. She was young but no fool. Michal was a woman in a time and place where your time and place were determined by men. She was sure that David would return to her soon. After all, she was Michal, daughter of Saul, the king of Israel.

However, as the days turned into weeks and the weeks into months, came the embarrassing realization that she had been abandoned. This was something Michal, daughter of Saul, would have never imagined from her "beloved" (the meaning of David's name).

When David escaped from Saul, he went to Ramah where the judge Samuel, who anointed him and previously Saul, lived. Ramah was not far from Gibeah.[14]

---

14   There are two Ramahs that scholars have debated on with reference to this text. There was a Ramah in the tribal territory of Benjamin. Also, there was Ramah of Ephraim where the prophet/judge Samuel was born. Ancient maps place this Ramah in the vicinity of Gibeah, the birthplace of Saul and the capital from which he ruled.

However, there was never an effort on David's part to go back to see Michal. God's Word writes of several meetings between David and Jonathan during his time as a fugitive. They spoke at length as friends, swearing loyalty to each other (1 Samuel 20:1-23, 35-43, 23:15-18), but David never inquired or spoke of his wife, who had helped save his life.

Michal may not have known the particulars, but knowing how close David and Jonathan were, no doubt she assumed they were in contact. How, she must have wondered, could David not ask about her? How could he not have given Jonathan a keepsake or pledge, a sign, a symbol of their love, something to assure her that he would return to her?

Over time, Michal begins to learn that one of the biggest clues that the relationship you claim to be in isn't all you claim it to be is when you're the one doing all the heavy lifting to keep it going.

Looking at the escape scene again, God's Word never records David looking back or saying anything to Michal as he made his escape, not even a thank you. There was no heartfelt goodbye, no plea to come with, and, more importantly, no promise to return or goodbye kiss, which would denote a relationship. Nothing.

From the beginning, it was a one-sided affair. Again, this is one of the few times Michal is described as David's wife. The good news is, at this point in their relationship, Michal was fulfilling the role of a wife by being a helpmate (Genesis 2:18). The bad news is that she was helping a hopeless cause.

1 Samuel 19:12 – …he fled and escaped.

David married Michal out of duty. He did not love her or even like her that much. It is interesting that one of the Hebrew meanings for the word "escape" is *malat,* which means "to be delivered." David not only escaped from Saul's murderous intentions, he also escaped a marriage he really didn't want to be in. He was delivered from being the lead character in Michal's self-produced romantic fantasy. He was delivered from the "on demand" performances of action hero her father could no longer do.

Note also that Michal had an identity as David's wife as she was trying to help and save him. Sometimes one has an identity in a relationship only when they're in the midst of trying to save it. Also, the validity of a relationship is measured by the amount of drama in it. Without the drama (manufactured or otherwise), the relationship is on life support.

By escaping through non-communication, non-involvement, etc., David signaled to Michal a DNR (do not resuscitate). But Michal, daughter of Saul, was loathe to admit the sad truth that the marriage was dead. Too proud, too stubborn, she continued to hold on to the fantasy of her and David together forever, just as she had imagined when she first saw him.

Instead of letting it die with dignity, Michal hooked her marriage to the ventilator of her fear of being alone, of losing direction of the script she wrote for her life that guaranteed a happy ending because, after all, she was Michal, daughter of Saul the king of Israel.

Michal was so wedded to the wedding that she failed to realize that her relationship and marriage to David lacked two key essentials that would define his relationships with the women who mattered the most to him—friendship and passion. With Abigail, you got a sense of deep friendship and respect. Theirs was a mutual admiration society.

1 Samuel 25:32–33 – David said to Abigail, "Praise be to the lord, the God of Israel, who has sent you today to meet me. May you be blessed for your good judgment and for keeping me from bloodshed this day and from avenging myself with my own hands."

Bathsheba, on the other hand, was simply "the one." She was David's great passion who grew to be the great love of his life. Over the years when God's promised reaping came from what he had sown by way of adultery, murder, and an attempted cover up (2 Samuel 11, 12:1-14), David never took out his frustrations or regrets on Bathsheba. He never blamed her for anything. David married Bathsheba not out of a sense of duty but because he truly and deeply loved her (2 Samuel 12:18-24).

A More Perfect Union

Years passed and by God's will, David survived Saul's numerous attempts to capture and kill him. Even though David passed up two opportunities to kill Saul (1 Samuel 24:1-10, 26:7-16), Saul's spiritual and mental instability prevented him from grasping the grace God was giving him. He continued to fight on, determined to hold on to his power and position that were gradually slipping away. *Proverbs 21:30 – There is no wisdom, no insight, no plan that can succeed against the Lord.*

He devised yet another scheme to stay on the throne. Saul engaged the help of a prominent Benjamite family headed by Laish (whose name means "lion") from Gallim, a village near Gibeah, Saul's hometown. Laish had a son by the name of Paltiel, which means "God delivers." Though bitter, depressed, paranoid, and in denial, Saul still had tremendous influence and power at his disposal, especially among his fellow tribesmen because of his position as king of Israel. He used this influence and power to arrange a marriage between Michal and Paltiel (1 Samuel 25:44).

Never one to let God's commands get in his way,[15] Saul forced Michal into an adulterous relationship by giving her hand in marriage to Paltiel despite the fact she was still married to David.[16]

Proverbs 19:21 – Many are the plans in a man's heart, but it is the Lord's purpose that prevails

In giving Michal to Paltiel, Saul attempted to solidify and broaden his political base among his fellow Benjamites and quell rumors among the other

---

15   Commandment number seven: *Exodus 20:14 – You shall not commit adultery.*
16   Whether David knew about this marriage, Scripture does not say. If he did, David could ponder the meaning of it all in the arms of Abigail who he had married despite still being married to Michal (*1 Samuel 25:39-40*).

tribes surrounding the stability of both him and his kingdom amidst David's increasing personal and political popularity.

Saul was not concerned about Michal's feelings. Saul was concerned about family. In marrying Paltiel, Saul also sought to provide Michal with a chance to have children. They would be the heirs to the dynasty he hoped to still have. It mattered little whether Michal was happily or miserably married. She was getting older. Saul needed to have grandchildren (the more the merrier), not to bounce on his knee, but to sit on the throne.

James 5:11 – The Lord is full of compassion and mercy.

Scripture never records Michal praying or calling on the Lord, but despite her spiritual insensitivity, God continued to show mercy and have compassion for her. First, Michal had the opportunity of knowing David, thus knowing and having a relationship with God. Now the Lord presented Michal with the opportunity to soothe her broken heart by giving her to a man who actually wanted to be with her (2 Samuel 3:16).

Saul had no idea that in arranging the marriage of Michal to Paltiel, he arranged for Michal to at last have a man who truly loved her for herself. In Paltiel, Michal was given the chance to be with a man who accepted her for who she was and what she had been through. Being the son of a powerful leader, Paltiel knew that marriages for political purposes happened all the time. Surely, coming from the same tribe, knowing Saul's family, Paltiel knew all about David and the Michal, David, and Saul love-hate triangle.

He knew the circumstances surrounding his marriage to Michal were less than ideal. A certificate of divorce as required by the Law of Moses (Deuteronomy 24:4) had not been presented to Michal from David. As far as the Law was concerned, by marrying Michal, *he* was committing adultery (Leviticus 20:10, Deuteronomy 22:22).

Paltiel also suffered no illusions. He knew if David came back, Michal would go to him…gladly. Surely Paltiel knew he could never measure up to David's military prowess and artistic expression. He knew he was second best. But then so was Michal. Her youth was fading. She had come to him full of disappointment and disillusion. But Palitel decided to love her anyway.

> *Love is hope, girl, love is strength.*
> *Here's someone standing right beside you*
> *who would go to any length to give you love true and deep*
> *and hope you realize at last you've found a love that you can keep*

—Baby, Baby Don't Cry, Smokey Robinson and the Miracles©

Paltiel is twice called something David is never called once in reference to Michal—*her husband*. Paltiel cared about Michal and not out of a sense of duty. Paltiel knew he couldn't fill David's shoes, but he wanted to walk with her anyway. Maybe Paltiel couldn't be the hero Michal wanted, but he could be the husband she needed.

The Bible does not give any additional biographical information about Paltiel. We do not know if he had been married previously. He may have been a widower. Palitel seemed like the kind of man who would never abandon or seek an escape from his wife.

But when given the choice of being happy with a man who seemed to love her unconditionally and one who, quite frankly, couldn't care less, Michal chose to hate David rather than love Paltiel.

David had abandoned her, but she still wanted to be with him—or thought she should be. Imagine that. After all these years, Michal couldn't let go. She still held on to that fairytale ending she had imagined years ago. After all, she was Michal, daughter of Saul, the king of Israel.

Maybe that is the reason God's Word never speaks of her having children by Paltiel. Although the bloom was off the rose, Michal still had the ability to bud. But for as long as she and Paltiel were married, as much as Paltiel loved her, maybe Michal just couldn't conceive of being with anyone else but David.

I play the game, a fantasy
I pretend I'm not in reality
I need the shelter of your arms to comfort me
No other sound is quite the same as your name
No touch can do half as much to make me feel better
So let's stay together....

—Ain't Nothing Like the Real Thing, Marvin Gaye and Tammi Terrell©

A Return Engagement

1 Samuel 14:52 – All the days of Saul there was bitter war with the Philistines...

No longer the hero Michal imagined him to be, no longer the man God anointed him to be, Saul, fearful and inept, led three of Michal's brothers to their death in his final fight against the Philistines.

1 Samuel 31:2-4 – The Philistines pressed hard after Saul and his sons, and they killed his sons Jonathan, Abinadab, and Malki-Shua. The fighting grew fierce around Saul, and when the archers overtook him, they wounded him critically. Saul said to his armor-bearer, "Draw your sword and run me through, or these uncircumcised fellows will come and run me through and abuse me." But his armor-bearer was terrified and would not do it; so Saul took his own sword and fell on it.

Saul's suicide was the period in a long sentence of self-destruction. Michal would have no idea of the confusion, horror, and fear both external and internal that surrounded her father at the end of his life. All that she knew was that her father died a hero—her hero.

2 Samuel 1:19, 22, 25 – Your glory, O Israel, lies slain on your heights. How the mighty have fallen!... From the blood of the slain, from the flesh of the mighty, the bow of Jonathan did not turn back, the sword of Saul did not return unsatisfied. ..How the mighty have fallen in battle!

With Saul dead, David was anointed first as king over the house of Judah (2 Samuel 2:4) and later as king over the entire house of Israel (2 Samuel 5:1- 4).

However, in the power vacuum that immediately followed Saul's death, Saul's cousin and the commander of his army, Abner—whose name means "the father is a lamp"—placed Saul's son Ish-Bosheth on the throne (1 Samuel 14:50, 2 Samuel 2:8-9). Ish-Bosheth—who would live up to the meaning of his name (man of shame)—was the fourth son of Saul. However, there is no mention of him until the death of his father and brothers. Pointedly, he was absent on that fateful day on Mt. Gilboa when Saul, Jonathan, Abinadab, and Malki-Shua were killed. During the reign of Saul, consistently punctuated with war, there is no mention of the apparently able-bodied Ish-Bosheth ever participating in battle.

Ish-Bosheth may have been the son of a woman other than Ahinoam since he was not included in the genealogy of Saul's family (1 Samuel 14:49–51).[17] Whoever his mother was, Ish-Bosheth inherited his father's tendency toward insecurity and timidity (2 Samuel 3:11, 4:1). By his own failings, Ish-Bosheth became merely a puppet king with Abner holding the strings (2 Samuel 3:6).

Ish-Bosheth took orders from the self-serving Abner in granting David's demand for the return of Michal as part of a peace treaty between the House of David and the House of Saul.

2 Samuel 3:12–14 – Then Abner sent messengers on his behalf to say to David, "Whose land is it? Make an agreement with me, and I will help you bring all Israel over to you." "Good," said David. "I will make an agreement with you. But I demand one thing of you. Do not come into my presence unless you bring Michal daughter of Saul when you come to see me." Then David sent messengers to Ish-Bosheth son of Saul, demanding, "Give me my wife Michal, who I betrothed to myself for the price of a hundred Philistine foreskins."

---

17 He is listed in Saul's genealogy in *1 Chronicles 8:33, 9:39* as *Esh-Baal.* 1 Chronicles provides a more extensive genealogy of the tribes, whereas the author of 1 Samuel put emphasis on the establishment of the Davidic dynasty.

The Bible does not say how long Paltiel and Michal were married by this time. Theirs couldn't have been the easiest of marriages, but it was a marriage where Michal could at least be herself or at least the self she best loved to be. Paltiel gave her the freedom to continue in the role she was most comfortable at playing—the beautiful, adored princess. Perhaps Michal wasn't happy, but at least she was at peace. But it was not to last.

2 Samuel 3:15-16 – So Ish-Bosheth gave orders and had her taken away from her husband Paltiel son of Laish. Her husband, however, went with her, weeping behind her all the way to Bahurim. Then Abner said to him "Go back home!" So he went back.

In spending the last moments with Michal before she was to be reunited with David, Paltiel took the unusual position (for a man) of walking behind Michal, a sign of subservience, in addition to weeping for her. In all of God's Word, there are only three times where it is written that a man weeps for a woman (this takes into account the words cry, cried, and wept - *NIV*): When Jacob arrives in Paddan Aram after running from Esau, he weeps when he sees and meets Rachel and the rest of his family that his mother (Rebekah) had sent him to (Genesis 29:10–12), and in the book of *Judges*, Jephthah, a mighty warrior, cries for the daughter he must sacrifice because of a vow he made with God (Judges 11:29–35).

And now we have Paltiel, crying after the woman with whom he thought he would be spending the rest of his life with, crying for the realization that what he had feared had come to pass—Michal was going back to David. He couldn't fight because he couldn't win. Paltiel was a man without power and a man without influence, and his wife knew it. So why should he care about his dignity? He wept.

God's Word does not write of Michal showing any emotion at this time. Nor does she seem to care about Paltiel's. Used by her father, abandoned by her husband, and now uprooted and used again as a pawn by that same husband and her only surviving brother, Michal had no tears left.

During the negotiations with Abner regarding her return, David initially described Michal not as his wife, but as "*the daughter of Saul*" to show respect and honor to the tribe of Benjamin and those still loyal to the House of Saul (2 Samuel 3:13). With her brother, Ish-Bosheth, David took a more forceful approach to emphasize the changing dynamics of power. Michal was not the daughter of Saul, but his wife.

As David's wife, Michal is now called upon again to help him. Though David is king, Michal is needed to save him. Years ago she wanted to, now she had to. This time, instead of helping him escape Saul, Michal was called upon to help David *escape* the political and spiritual suspicions (especially among her tribe of Benjamin) surrounding the validity of David's right to rule. David needed Michal as a symbol of the United Kingdom of Israel—the unity between the House of Saul and the House of David. Michal was called upon to be that wife—that political wife—standing by her man with a wave and a smile.

How cruel, how utterly cruel it must have been for Michal to find herself being wanted for all the wrong reasons. As she prepared to meet David, Michal knew it wasn't out of love that he had sent for her. That should have happened years ago.

This would be the third and final time Michal would be used as a chess piece by the men of her family—her father, her brother, and now by David. It had come full circle. Saul used Michal to strengthen his hold on the throne, now her husband was doing the same thing. Thinking back to when she first saw him...funny she would have never imagined something like this.

2 Samuel 6:12 – ...So David went down and brought up the ark of God from the house of Obed-Edom to the City of David with rejoicing.

The years of war with the Philistines were over. The years of war between the tribes were finally over. There was rejoicing in the land because of the victory God had given His people with David as their king. After so much blood, at last there was peace. It was a time to rejoice. However, as the sounds of celebration drifted through the window of David's home, where Michal had been brought, Michal probably wondered what on earth she had to celebrate.

All the excitement about the return of the ark seemed to throw salt into past wounds still raw with remembrance. Michal knew about the Ark symbolizing God's presence[18] . But it was a presence that seemed to have alluded Michal all of her life. Frankly all this rejoicing was getting on her nerves. The singing, the tambourines, all reminded her of a happier time so distant now. Michal knew she should be happy, at least for the nation. But she wasn't. She couldn't be. Michal, daughter of Saul, probably never felt so out of place. By this time, she had been so disappointed and so disgusted with life that she couldn't see that she was now in a good place at a good time.

Isaiah 43:18-19 – Forget the former things; do not dwell on the past. See, I am doing a new thing! Now it springs up; do you not perceive it?

The only thing Michal could understand was that nothing had happened as she had imagined. The phrase "past imperfect" meant little to Michal, because in her mind her past was perfect. Her father was alive and *he* was the king. Her

---

18   Also called the Ark of the Covenant, the ark of God, the ark of the Lord and the ark of the Testimony, it was the most sacred object of the Israelites during this time. It contained the two stone tablets of the Ten Commandments, a pot of manna, and Aaron's rod that budded (*Exodus: 16:33, 25:16, Numbers17:1-11*). After it was captured by the Philistines and subsequently returned to the Israelites (*1Samuel 4:22, 5, 6 7:1*), the ark remained Kiriath Jearim in the territory of Benjamin until David had it moved to Jerusalem.

brothers were alive. She had her big sister, Merab. Who knew if she was alive or dead? [19] Who would Michal ask and who would really care?

2 Samuel 6:14-15 – David, wearing a linen ephod, danced before the Lord with all his might, while he and the entire house of Israel brought up the Ark of the Lord with shouts and the sound of the trumpets.

As the celebration came closer, the more annoyed Michal became. When she finally decided to look out and saw the dancers, her husband being one of them, her blood began to boil. The dancing brought her to that place and time when she had first fallen for David, when he was *her hero*. It reminded Michal of the last time she had been truly happy. Now everything had changed and from her point of view, not for the better.

1 Samuel 18:7, 16 – As they danced, they sang: "Saul has slain his thousands, and David his tens of thousands."…all Israel and Judah loved David, because he led them in their campaigns.

As usual, Michal noticed that the women were drawn to him. So much time had passed, which probably brought to mind another loss Michal had suffered—that of her youth. By this time Michal was in her mid to late 20s—practically middle aged by the standards of the day. Seeing her husband after all those years, Michal may have been sensitive about her looks. It's intriguing that as the daughter of Saul whom the Bible describes as good looking (1 Samuel 9:2) and whose mother (Ahinoam) is assumed to have been beautiful as well, Michal is never described as such.

---

19   After Saul goes back on his promise to give Merab's hand in marriage to David as a reward for killing Goliath, Merab is not mentioned until early in David's reign as king of Israel. Unlike her young sister, Merab married and had at least five sons, which David had killed to avenge the Gibeonites who Saul had tried to exterminate (*2Samuel 21:2-9*).

One of the Hebrew words for beautiful is *naah,* which means "pleasant." Another Hebrew word for beautiful is *tiph-arah,* which means "ornament." One Greek definition for the word is *horaios,* means "flourishing" and "beauteous." Pointedly, Michal meant none of these things to David.

> *A pretty face may be some guys taste, but I'll take lovin' in its place*
> *'cuz I know that beauty's only skin deep yeah, yeah, yeah*
> *Beauty's only skin deep oh yeah...*
>
> *—Beauty's Only Skin Deep, The Temptations©*

However God's word described Abigail and Bathsheba as such...

1 Samuel 25:3 – His name was Nabal and his wife's name was Abigail. She was an intelligent and beautiful woman...

2 Samuel 11:2–3 – One evening David got up from his bed and walked around on the roof of the palace. From the roof he saw a woman bathing. The woman was very beautiful, and David sent someone to find out about her. The man said, "Isn't this Bathsheba..."

These and other women were beautiful in ways Michal could never be.[20]

Also, by this time, Michal most likely knew of David's other's wives, all six of them, as well as the children he had brought from Hebron to Jerusalem (2 Samuel 3:2-5).[21] For Michal, daughter of Saul, it was yet another blow to her ego. It was yet another bitter pill to swallow that although she was David's first

---

20 There was also the beautiful Abishag, recruited to attend to the aged King David (*1 Kings 1:1-4*)

21 Before moving the capital of the United Nation of Israel to Jerusalem, David ruled from Hebron for seven years (*2 Samuel 5:4-5*).

wife, she wasn't his first love nor did she birth his first child. This was not the way it was supposed to be. This was not how she imagined it at all.

As Michal pondered all of this, David was so caught up in the agony and ecstasy of the fulfillment of God's promise not only to him but the nation, that he broke all manner of custom and decorum by dancing in celebration of the return of the Ark of the Covenant.[22] The journey from pasture to throne: the running, the fighting, the wars and rumors of wars were over. It was a new day.

Ironically this was where Michal had always wanted to be—at home with David, but there was one exception, she was in Jerusalem not Gibeah, her home where her father reigned when *he* was king of Israel. This is the one truth out of all the hard truths that was probably hardest for Michal to accept. David would have always been a prince, her prince, while one of her brothers—no doubt Jonathan—would have succeeded Saul as king. That's how she had imagined it. That's the way it should have been. But, here she was, Michal, daughter of Saul, now totally dependent on a man who used to herd sheep.

2 Samuel 6:16 – As the ark of the Lord was entering the City of David, Michal daughter of Saul watched from a window. And when she saw King David leaping and dancing before the Lord, she despised him in her heart.

Instead of celebrating, he should be worshipping the ground she walked on, kissing her feet after all she had done for him. Lest anyone forget, she saved his life! At the very least he should be saying the words she had been waiting for him to say all these years: "I'm sorry." But instead David danced. He danced in spite of her pain and suffering. Her father and brothers were dead. Her life had

---

22 In the male-dominated culture of this time, dancing was almost exclusively done by women. The very word "dancing" in Hebrew—chagag—means to observe a festival. Women danced primarily for two reasons regarding a festival: to celebrate an Israelite victory in battle or during one of the great feasts and festivals held throughout the year by the Word of God (*Exodus 23:14-17*).

been turned upside down, inside out over and over again. Where was Merab? How in God's name could he dance?

Psalm 69:20 – Scorn has broken my heart and has left me helpless; I looked for sympathy, but there was none, for comforters, but I found none.

The Bitter End

2 Samuel 6:20 – When David returned home to bless his household, Michal daughter of Saul came out to meet him and said, "How the king of Israel has distinguished himself today, disrobing in the sight of slave girls of his servants as any vulgar fellow would!"

At their first real chance to talk since Michal was returned to him, this should have been an opportunity for the both of them to chart a new course in their relationship. Yet what greeted David wasn't the opportunity to start fresh and move on, but a stark reminder of why he never looked back after he escaped that night in Gibeah so long ago.

Job 7:11 – "Therefore, I will not keep silent; I will speak out in the anguish of my spirit, I will complain in the bitterness of my soul."

God's Word identified Michal at this crucial time not as David's wife, but all throughout the reunion section of the narrative as Michal, daughter of Saul. David requested his "wife," but instead got daddy's girl, still pathologically clinging to her idols, which were her past and her position.

1 Corinthians 13:11 – When I was a child, I talked like a child, I thought like a child, I reasoned like a child. When I became a man, I put childish ways behind me.

It was Michal, daughter of Saul, looking down on the celebration from the window (2 Samuel: 6:16). It was Michal, daughter of Saul, who confronted David one final time (2 Samuel 6:20). The circumstances of her family and her family's place in the nation had drastically changed. Her relationship with David had certainly changed. However, the way Michal saw herself had not. In her mind she was first the daughter of Saul and David's wife second. Of the

17 Scripture references in 1 and 2 Samuel over half (8) describe her as "Michal, daughter of Saul." In Biblical times, a woman's identity was derived from her relationship to a man. It is interesting and quite revealing to see which man Michal preferred to be identified with first.

2 Samuel 6:21–22 –David said to Michal, "It was before the Lord, who chose me rather than your father or anyone from his house when he appointed me ruler over the Lord's people Israel – I will celebrate before the Lord. I will become even more undignified than this, and I will be humiliated in my own eyes. But by these slave girls you spoke of, I will be held in honor."

This is the only time Scripture records David speaking directly to Michal. And it is one of the most emotionally charged encounters between a man and woman in the Bible.

Reunited and it feel so good
Reunited 'cuz we understood
There's one perfect fit, and sugar this one is it
We both are so excited 'cuz we're reunited, hey-hey

–Reunited, Peaches and Herb©

Michal had started the argument in a way most arguments are started. Ostensibly it's about what's happening in the present, but in reality it's all about the past. All her talk about the dancing can be translated into, "And another thing, you never came back for me."

In their final meeting, the level of animosity David felt toward Michal was quite apparent. Once upon a time, he may have been intrigued by her. Once upon a time, he may have been a bit in awe of her, after all, she was the daughter of Saul. But "once upon a time" is over, and now it's the end—the bitter end.

David retaliated by hitting Michal where it hurt, her misplaced pride. David spelled it out to her, very clearly, why the changing of the guard had taken place.

2 Samuel 6:21 – David said to Michal, "It was before the Lord, who chose me rather than your father or anyone from his house when he appointed me ruler over the Lord's people Israel."

Saul was dead. He was the king. Furthermore, he wasn't that naïve, shepherd boy having to prove himself to Saul, to her, or to anyone else. It's clear to David by Michal's attitude and remarks that she felt being the wife of God's anointed servant wasn't a blessing but a come down. And since that was the case, he would enjoy the company of women, men, and anybody else who was not ashamed to give God true genuine praise. The truth and nothing but the truth was that he never loved her, barely liked her, and now he couldn't stand the sight of her and would not tolerate her being in his presence ever again.

2 Samuel 6:23 – And Michal, daughter of Saul, had no children to the day of her death.

And so it is, the end of a long, painful journey for Michal, living out her days in opposition to God's Holy Word by being unproductive. Michal's failure to form a meaningful relationship with David simply symbolized her failure at forming a meaningful relationship with God.

John 15:5 – I am the vine; you are the branches. If a man remains in me and I in him, he will bear much fruit; apart from me you can do nothing.

Michal lived out her days in resentment, mad at the world and the one who made it over what came to be instead of what might have been.

She never learned the lesson that the past is a point of reference. It is not to be revisited or relived over and over again. Michal continually lived her life in rewind, which prevented her from having hope in God's coming attractions.

So she turned down any and all opportunities God presented her to experience His love, mercy, and grace. God's Word records her identity in the end not as David's wife, Israel's greatest king, the root of Jesse who would bring forth the Messiah. No, in the end, Michal was identified with a man who, like her, started out with so much but ended up with so little. Who would have imagined?

Job 17:11 – My days have passed, my plans are shattered, and so are the desires of my heart.

Leah

WHAT YOU SEE IS WHAT YOU GET

Leah

Mark 8:18 – Do you have eyes but fail to see, and ears but fail to hear?

Leah's name means "gazelle," an animal that the people of that time admired for both its delicate beauty and swiftness. In Hebrew the word for gazelle is *Tabitha* and in Arabic, it means "affectionate." But God's Word describes Leah as such:

Genesis 29:17 – Leah had weak eyes....

Leah was neither an ugly woman nor a sickly woman. After all, she birthed seven children. However, Leah did have a problem with her vision and that affected how she saw herself and everyone else, especially one man in particular. From the beginning, it was love at first sight but not for her.

Wedded Bliss

Genesis 29:9-10 – While he was talking with them Rachel came with her father's sheep, for she was a shepherdess. When Jacob saw Rachel, daughter of Laban, his mother's brother, and Laban's sheep, he went over and rolled the stone away from the mouth of the well and watered his uncle's sheep.

Genesis 29:18 – Jacob was in love with Rachel and said, "I'll work for you seven years in return for your younger daughter Rachel." [23]

The moment Jacob saw Leah's younger sister Rachel, which means "lamb," he was attracted to her. Rachel's pull was so strong that this introverted man (Genesis 25:27) found himself doing something he had never done before... work... in the great outdoors, helping to care for Laban's (whose name means "white") flocks and herds. The only payment Jacob wanted was Rachel.

Genesis 29:20 – So Jacob served seven years to get Rachel, but they seemed like only a few days to him because of his love for her.

Now during those seven years, Jacob never gave Leah a second look. He only had eyes for Rachel. Leah probably couldn't see why this was so since she and Jacob seemed much more alike. Like Jacob, but unlike Rachel, Leah was a quiet type of person, preferring to be inside... watching. Over the seven years, as she watched Jacob fall deeper and deeper in love with her sister, Leah no doubt wondered what it would be like to have that kind of love for herself. She really didn't have to wonder too much. It was staring her right in the face. It was the way Jacob looked at her sister.

---

23 Leah and Rachel were Jacob's cousins. During Biblical times and especially during the time of the Old Testament, marriages between relatives were not uncommon. The Mosaic Law put emphasis on marrying within the person's tribe and/or clan (*Exodus 34:10, Deuteronomy 7:3-4*). Marriage among cousins was not considered incestuous (*Leviticus 18:1-17*)

Genesis 29:21 – Then Jacob said to Laban, "Give me my wife. My time is completed, and I want to lie with her."

As Rachel's wedding approached, God's Word doesn't write of any suitors for Leah. As matrimony grew closer as a reality for Rachel, it remained a distant dream for Leah. Seven years had passed. Leah wasn't getting any younger. Something had to be done.

> *Last chance, last dance for love*
> *Yes, it's my last chance for romance tonight…*
> *Yeah will you be my Mr. Right?*
> *Can you fill my appetite?*
> *I can't be sure that you're the one for me*
> *But all I ask is that you dance with me*
> *Dance with me, dance with me, yeah*
>
> *–Last Dance, Donna Summer©*

Genesis 29:22-23 – So Laban brought together all the people of the place and gave a feast. But when evening came, he took his daughter Leah and gave her to Jacob and Jacob lay with her.

During Biblical times especially during the Old Testament, wedding festivities lasted for days. There was always plenty of food and wine, which flowed freely from beginning to end. Jacob probably drank with abandon. He had worked so long and so hard. No more looking, imagining what it would be like to be with her, to really be with her. The wait was over. At last he would be able to make love to the woman he had loved since the moment they first met. Drink up!

Proverbs 23:30-33 – Those who linger over wine, who go to sample bowls of mixed wine. Do not gaze at wine when it is red, when it sparkles in the cup, when it goes down smoothly! In the end it bites like a snake and poisons like a viper. Your eyes will see strange sights and your mind imagine confusing things.

While Jacob drank, Laban watched and saw the answer to the question of what to do about Leah. As Jacob had done to his twin brother, Esau, years earlier, now his father-in-law does to him (Genesis 25:29-34). Laban took advantage of a hunger. He knew Jacob was starved and he knew it wasn't for food.

Genesis 29:25 – When morning came, there was Leah! So Jacob said to Laban, "What is this you have done to me? I served you for Rachel, didn't I? Why have you deceived me?

Never mind the pot calling the kettle black aspect of this conversation regarding deception. Laban calmly explained the custom of giving the oldest daughter in marriage first. Laban was not telling Jacob anything new given his own family history, particularly with his brother, Esau. He was just telling Jacob something he didn't want to hear.

But there was something else. Though much of the night had been a blur, Jacob did remember one thing. Leah's uninhibited and grateful lovemaking was something Jacob couldn't forget. He'd be deceiving himself if he didn't admit to himself how good Leah was in bed.

Surely My Husband Will Love Me Now

Leviticus 18:18 – Do not take your wife's sister as a rival wife and have sexual relations with her while your wife is living.

Despite Jacob's and Leah's tremendous sexual chemistry, Jacob's feelings for Rachel went beyond the physical. Laban knew this and used Jacob's feelings for Rachel to his advantage. With a firm grasp on Jacob's Achilles heel[24] (his love for Rachel), Laban dangled the promise of marriage to Rachel to hold him to another seven years of labor (Genesis 29:26-27).

Genesis 29:28-30 – …He finished the week with Leah, and then Laban gave him his daughter Rachel to be his wife. Laban gave his servant girl Bilhah to his daughter Rachel as her maidservant. Jacob lay with Rachel also and he loved Rachel more than Leah. And he worked for Laban another seven years.

Earlier Laban had given his other servant girl Zilpah to Leah (Genesis 29:24). So, within a week Jacob had four women at his "*bed* and call".[25]

1 Corinthians 14:33 (KJV) – For God is not the author of confusion but of peace, as in all churches of the saints.

It was more than a poor boy from Beersheba could have imagined (Genesis 28:10). Not only did Jacob have Rachel, the love of his life, but he had the lusts of his life as well. If Zilpah or Bilhah or even Leah thought he felt anything for them, well they were only deceiving themselves.

---

24   More turnabout as it goes back to Jacob and Esau's birth. Esau came out first but Jacob came out "grasping Esau's heel" (*Genesis 25:26*).

25   Zilpah and Bilhah were female slaves. Women slaves during this time were often used as sexual partners for their masters as permitted by the Law. They were used as sexual gifts, given to the master's sons or his friends. The word concubine is the formal definition of what Zilpah and Bilhah were. *Genesis 35:22* calls Bilhah Jacob's concubine.

Proverbs 27:7 – He who is full loathes honey, but to the hungry even what is bitter tastes sweet.

If Jacob made no secret about his feeling for Rachel, he was just as emphatic about his feelings for Leah: "*he finished the week with her.*" After seven days Jacob was completely through acting as a husband. For Leah, after seven days and nights, she was completely in love and lust. Yes, he had looked at her with disgust and disappointment the morning after, but it was after the night she had felt "love" and gave love. It was after she had been held and caressed. Whatever came after was better than the before of loneliness and frustration that Leah had felt all these years before that night.

> *I remember not too long ago*
> *I was just a lonely person with a lonely heart*
> *And I was hopin' there could one day be*
> *Be a chance for me to*
> *Get the love that I'd been missin'*
> *Sometimes love takes a long time…*
>
> *–Wait for Love, Luther Vandross©*

In his own way, the maestro of this mess—her father, Laban—was looking out for Leah. The times said that a woman was nothing without a man, even if having one robbed her of her dignity and worth. It was only when a woman was married that she had an identity. And speaking of identity, Laban could not be identified as a failure as a father because of his inability to arrange a marriage for Leah. The stigma of Leah's single status was casting a pall over the entire family and ruining his reputation as a mover and a shaker. Laban couldn't have his power and position questioned because of Leah. So he did what he had to do.

Genesis 29:23. ...he took his daughter Leah and gave her to Jacob and Jacob lay with her.

Of the many words in Hebrew for the word "took", one, *gazal*, means "to rob." The marriage Laban arranged for Leah would further rob her of the self-esteem she hoped to get by being married in the first place.

However, with Rachel, Laban's actions are described differently, because his feelings for Rachel are different. She was his favorite. While the Bible says Laban *"took"* Leah, in regards to the nuptials between Jacob and Rachel, Scripture says *"and then Laban gave him (Jacob) his daughter Rachel to be his wife." (Genesis 29:23).* One of the Hebrew words for "gave" is *yacaph*, meaning to add or augment. Rachel added love to Jacob's life. His love for her made him unselfish and hardworking. With Rachel, Jacob would do anything and give anything for her. With Leah it was all take away.

Genesis 29:32 – ...Surely my husband will love me now.

Leah said these words after she gave birth to her firstborn, Reuben. For Leah, the birth of Reuben may have meant her relationship with Jacob could turn a corner from being primarily physical in nature. After all, she, not Rachel, had given birth to his first child; a son.[26]

Genesis 29:34 – ...Now at last my husband will become attached to me, because I have borne him three sons. So she named him Levi.

The birth of Reuben is followed by Simeon and Levi. How could Jacob not love her now? She had given him three healthy sons. Rachel hadn't even gotten pregnant (Genesis 29:31, 30:1).

After three sons, why wouldn't Jacob love her more, since she, and not Rachel, had proven to him what a potent lover he was (Deuteronomy 21:17). Why wouldn't Jacob love her more, since she not Rachel had now given him a

---

26 A family's heritage and inheritance was preserved through sons.

family to fill the void of the one he had left years ago? Now that he had sons to carry on his name, he wouldn't have to wander anymore.[27] He had a home with her and their sons. Surely he would love her now.

Psalm 127:3-5 – Sons are a heritage from the Lord, children a reward from him. Like arrows in the hands of a warrior are sons born in one's youth. Blessed is the man whose quiver is full of them.

Leah hoped the children would help deepen their relationship on a vertical plane. Yet for all the babies, the Bible doesn't record these two having a single conversation. For Jacob, the die was cast the night of the wedding. Their relationship wasn't about talking. He talked to one woman. He bore his soul to one woman. With Leah there was no need to talk. Jacob knew what she wanted. What more was there to say?

---

27 *Genesis 28:5, Deuteronomy 26:5 – My father was a wandering Aramean..* is a reference to Jacob who had wandered from his home in Canaan to Aram where he marries Leah and Rachel: Aramean women.

The Hand the Rocks the Cradle[28]

Genesis 30:1-2 – When Rachel saw that she was not bearing Jacob any children, she became jealous of her sister. So she said to Jacob, "Give me children or I'll die." Jacob became angry with her and said, "Am I in the place of God, who has kept you from having children?"

As much as God's Word says Jacob loved Rachel, the only conversation Scripture records these two having (like Michal and David) is in the form of an argument. It's an argument full of jealousy, fear, threats, and uncertainty. It was an honest conversation between two people not used to being honest with anyone.

For Jacob, loving Rachel was never easy. She was bossy, scheming, and manipulative. She was also a thief (Genesis 31:19). In many respects, she was like another bossy, scheming, and manipulative woman Jacob knew. In many ways, Rachel was a younger and prettier version of his mom, Rebekah. Be that as it may, despite Rachel's faults, or maybe because of them, Jacob adored her, whether she had children or not. She infuriated and infatuated him at the same time.

> *Every time I think I've had enough, I start heading for the door.*
> *There's a very strange vibration piercing me right to the core.*
> *It says turn around you fool you know you love her more and more*
> *Tell me why is it so. Don't wanna let you go.*

> *–Never Can Say Goodbye, The Jackson 5©*

---

28 A South African Proverb: "The hand that rocks the cradle rules the nation and its destiny". Also a poem by American poet William Ross Wallace (1819 – 1881) *The Hand That Rocks the Cradle is the Hand that Rules the World.* Both the proverb and the poem emphasize the tremendous influence mothers have in shaping the citizenry of a nation and thus determining its destiny.

When he first met Rachel, she was coming in from herding and caring for her father's sheep (Genesis 29:6-11). No doubt she was dirty, sweaty, and smelly. But as soon as Jacob saw this dirty, smelly woman, he offered to help her. He wanted to help her. He needed to help her. Rachel, on the other hand, didn't ask him to and never thanked him when he did. Scripture says Jacob's response was to do something to Rachel he never did to Leah—he kissed her.

Genesis 29:10-11 – When Jacob saw Rachel daughter of Laban, his mother's brother, and Laban's sheep, he went over and rolled the stone away from the mouth of the well and watered his uncle's sheep. Then Jacob kissed Rachel and began to weep aloud.

Romantic kisses are rarely mentioned in the Bible, but kisses, whether platonic or arduous, do denote one thing—a close relationship. Maybe it was love. Maybe it was lust. Maybe it was both. But the moment Jacob saw Rachel, he felt a close relationship with her. Though Leah was the first wife and birthed him more children than any other woman, Jacob never felt close to her.

But oh the chemistry, so…

Genesis 29:35 – She conceived again and when she gave birth to a son she said, "This time I will praise the Lord." So she named him Judah. Then she stopped having children.

This was the first time that Leah named a child without attaching Jacob or her situation with Jacob to the child. Unlike the other children who were named after her need for Jacob's love and approval (Genesis 29:32-34), this fourth child was named after the proper response for God's love and mercy toward her—Judah which means praise.[29]

---

29 The tribe from which Jacob would later prophesize the Messiah, Jesus Christ would come from (*Genesis 49:8-12*).

Meanwhile, for the first time in her life, Rachel was contending with the fact of being second to her sister, at least when it came to having children. This was not good. Rachel was not used to being second to anybody or anything. She was used to having her way and like her father and husband, she would use anybody to get it.

Genesis 30:3 – Then she said, "Here is Bilhah, my maidservant. Sleep with her so that she can bear children for me and that through her I too can build a family."

Taking a page from Sarai (Sarah), Rachel showed how different she viewed having children from her sister. [30] With the exception of Reuben, whenever Leah had a child (as well as her maidservant, Zilpah), God's Holy Word (NIV) says she "conceived" prior to giving birth. On the other hand, with Joseph and Benjamin, the Bible says Rachel either gave or gives *"birth"* (Genesis 30:22-23, 35:16). The Hebrew word for "conceive" is *harah*, which simply means "to be pregnant" or *zara*, which means "to sow seed, disseminate." One Hebrew meaning for the word birth is *towl dah* meaning "family descent, family of record."

In getting pregnant and having Jacob's children, Leah saw a chance to get the love she always wanted. The children were the seeds Leah sowed so she might reap Jacob's love and affection.

Rachel, on the other hand, saw in Bilhah an opportunity to attain the power that a woman at that time got from having children. Secure in Jacob's love, Rachel didn't need children so much to please her husband but to empower herself. The children would give her even more control over Jacob

---

30   Sarai, Abram's wife also suffered the societal embarrassment of being barren. Rather than wait for God's promise of a child of their own (*Genesis 15:4-5*), Sarai with Abram's approval employs Hagar, Sarai's maidservant, to be a surrogate mother (*Genesis 16:1-2*).

than she already had. Power and control, that's what Rachel wanted and that's something Leah never really *conceived* of.

> *I'm in control, never gonna stop*
> *Control, to get what I want*
> *Control, I like to have a lot*
> *Control now I'm all grown up*
>
> *—Control, Janet Jackson©*

Genesis 30:3 (KJV) – "And she said, Behold my maid Bilhah, go in unto her; and she shall bear upon my knees, that I may also have children by her."

The statement Rachel made, *"she shall bear upon my knees,"* symbolizes adoption. Jacob would later do this with his grandsons: Manasseh and Ephraim of his favorite son Joseph (Genesis 48:8-12).

This shepherdess, who was used to being outside and not confined to anyone's perception of what she could and could not do, used the language and imagery usually reserved for men.

Luke 16:8 – For the people of this world are more shrewd in dealing with their own kind than are the people of light.

In using Bilhah as a surrogate mother, Rachel proved once again that she was her father's daughter. When she realized she was having problems getting pregnant, Rachel offered Jacob Bilhah, her maidservant. Bilhah's name means "unconcerned." There would be no Abraham-Hagar-Sarah drama. Rachel would see to that. She was in control.

Now all this time, Leah was praising God and busy raising the four sons she already had. Then she found out about Rachel's plans.

Genesis 30:9 – When Leah saw that she stopped having children, she took her maidservant Zilpah and gave her to Jacob as a wife.

Although leading with a ratio of four to one, Leah's insecurity kept her from keeping her focus on God. She knew that babies and the process of making them was her trump card with Jacob. And now with the threat of Rachel's proxy giving birth, Leah felt she had no other choice but to play it again.

Galatians 4:9 – But now that you know God – or rather are known by God – how is it that you are turning back to those weak and miserable principles? Do you wish to be enslaved by them all over again?

Leah allowed her fears—rooted in low to no self-esteem—to rule her. She went back to doing the very things that kept her in the very situation that made her so very unhappy in the first place.

Genesis 30:10-13 – Leah's servant Zilpah bore Jacob a son. Then Leah said, "What good fortune!" So she named him Gad. Leah's servant Zilpah bore Jacob a second son. Then Leah said, "How happy I am. The women will call me happy." So she named him Asher.

Mama's Boy

The women in the vicinity probably called Leah many things, but happy would not necessarily be one of them. Everyone knew that Rachel was the favored wife. Couldn't Leah see that? Couldn't she see that with four women at his disposal, if anyone could be called happy; it would have to be Jacob?

In addition to these and other delusions, Leah couldn't see how her behavior, her attitude, and her view of herself affected her children. Blinded by her obsession for Jacob, she couldn't see how they both had sown seeds of dysfunction that would disseminate throughout the family for generations to come. [31] When it came to Jacob, Leah subscribed to the strategy "by any means necessary." She used herself and she used the children. She used the children to bolster her esteem and mask the self-hatred Jacob's rejection of her (outside the bedroom) caused.

The children became the sacrifices Leah offered on the altar of her love for Jacob. Both Leah and Jacob willingly sacrificed their children's view of a happy marriage and a loving family. Their children never saw a healthy relationship between their parents. Day after day, year after year, Leah's children never saw their mother happy unless their father was around, which was more out of convenience rather than conviction. They saw their mother swing from delirium over having a baby to desperately wanting another one…for him.

Genesis 29:31-32 – When the Lord saw that Leah was not loved; he opened her womb, but Rachel was barren. Leah became pregnant and gave birth to a son. She named him Reuben for she said, "It is because the Lord has seen my misery. Surely my husband will love me now."

---

31 See page 50 for the Hebrew word for conceive; pregnant.

The Lord wasn't the only one to see that Leah was not loved, so did her children, starting with her firstborn, Reuben. His name means "behold a son." He was the one who was to have made it all better. Because of his position as the firstborn and arguably the son closest to her, Reuben had a front row seat to his parent's personal drama. Reuben was both Leah's son and *quasi husband*. Whenever Jacob wasn't around, which was often, there was Reuben to confide in. Through no fault of his own, Reuben became more familiar than he should have with his mother and father's dysfunctional relationship. He grew up watching his mother's preoccupation with loving a man who didn't love her but loved using her—a man who just happened to be his father. And something else, Reuben never really saw his father happy unless he was with another woman, his aunt Rachel. Reuben saw it all, and it was all too much.

As the oldest son, Reuben probably often thought there must be something he could or should do since one day he would be responsible for leading the family.

Genesis 30:14 – During wheat harvest, Reuben went out into the fields and found some mandrake plants which he brought to his mother Leah.

The wheat harvest, like all the other agricultural harvests in Biblical times, was a festive occasion. It was also a very significant time since wheat was one of the most important plants that grew in Israel. It was the main ingredient for bread—a staple of the Hebrew diet and of worship services.[32]

The wheat harvest occurred in the spring (April/May). Reuben—the compassionate brother, the one who would later persuade his other brothers in their jealousy not to kill Joseph (Genesis 37:21-22), who would pledge his own sons as security for Benjamin (the only other son by Jacob's beloved wife Rachel)

---

32   The Showbread or Bread of Presence (*Leviticus 24:5-9*) that was kept in the temple, symbolized God's presence and provision toward His people. The Passover was commemorated by eating unleavened bread (*Exodus 12:17-2*). Jesus calls himself "The Bread of Life" (*John 6:32-33*).

on a second trip to Egypt during a famine (Genesis 42:36-37)—wanted to help his mother. If he helped her, he would help himself and the family because perhaps then she wouldn't complain and fuss so much around him and his brothers. Perhaps, for once, *he* could make her happy.

One of the Hebrew words for "found" is *chagar,* meaning "to examine, to search." Reuben didn't just stumble upon the mandrakes—a plant from the potato family that produces yellow sweet-tasting fruit.[33] He was actively looking for them.

How did Reuben know about mandrakes? His mother told him. Why was Reuben looking for a sometime-narcotic, sometime-aphrodisiac plant at this crucial time when wheat needed to be harvested? Why did he take a break from the camaraderie of his friends or perhaps a young lady to look for mandrakes? Why? Because his mama wanted him to.

Leah is often painted as the poor, put-upon sister—"victim" is thy name. But here we see a different Leah, a selfish Leah, willing to use her son to keep her man, willing to sacrifice her son's needs and the community's needs for her own. In her desperation, Leah couldn't see herself acting just like her father, just like her husband—just like all the people who had used her before.

Leah's obsession for Jacob had escalated to the point where it interfered with her children's lives. It prevented them from having one. Scripture does not say if Reuben was married at that time. He was certainly of the age to be or, with his father's approval, looking to be.[34] It was spring, when a young man's

---

33 The roots of the plants bear a resemblance to a human body. During this time, the root of the plant was used to promote conception. In addition to being used as an aphrodisiac, the root of the mandrake plant is said to have a narcotic quality.

34 According to Jewish tradition there are four specific duties that a father is to have toward his son(s): to have them circumcised, to pass on his inheritance to the firstborn (*Deuteronomy 21:17*), to teach them a trade, and find wives for them.

thoughts should turn to love. At a time when Reuben should have been about the business of getting a love life of his own, he was aiding and abetting his mother's. Reuben couldn't be his own man because he was trying to help his mother keep one. It was emotional incest.

Reuben spent all his childhood and young adulthood listening and watching his mother twist and turn herself inside out over his father. This preoccupation with his parents' issues may have been one of the reasons Reuben never felt the sense of privilege and purpose that usually comes with being the eldest son, "the first sign of his father's strength" (Deuteronomy 21:15-17). All his life, Reuben, along with his siblings, watched as all the attention their father should have given them lavished on another woman and her children, despite all that their mother had done.

During his formative years, Reuben watched his father come and go when and after he was pleased. All his life he watched his mother accept the piece of a relationship she had with his father. All his life he witnessed and felt his mother's second-class status, her powerlessness over her own emotions. As an adult, Reuben would come to reap what his parents had sowed. He would tragically come to identify with the same kind of "on the outside looking in" mentality that Leah had, in essence, groomed him to have.

Genesis 35:22 – While Israel was living in that region, Reuben went in and slept with his father's concubine Bilhah, and Israel heard of it.

What is interesting is that Reuben didn't sleep with Leah's maidservant, Zilpah, but Rachel's maidservant, Bilhah.

Leviticus 18:8 – Do not have sexual relations with your father's wife; that would dishonor your father.

With one act, Reuben vindicated his mother and condemned his father at the same time, all in the arms of Bilhah. She would act as proxy for Rachel. He couldn't sleep with her so Bilhah, her maidservant, was the next best thing.

Over the years, Reuben learned the lesson from his parents to take his pleasure when and where he found it. Unlike his mother, he wouldn't make the mistake of waiting for things to get better. By watching his mother and *father*, Reuben learned to "live for the moment," for if tomorrow comes there's a good chance it will look just like yesterday. Reuben wouldn't wait for his father to die to have his pleasure. He had seen his mother wait, so waiting was out of the question. His pleasure would be derived not only from sexual gratification but something else more visceral—revenge. Reuben would take the authority his mother never could and signal to his father and family how he really felt after all those years.

Reuben's love-hate relationship with his parents had him riding a roller coaster of emotions that he could never quite come to terms with. And on his deathbed, Jacob unknowingly prophesied the impact of Reuben's involuntary ownership of the psychodrama he and Leah produced.

Genesis 49:3-4 – "Reuben you are my firstborn, my might, the first sign of my strength, excelling in honor, excelling in power. Turbulent as the waters, you will no longer excel, for you went up onto your father's bed, onto my couch and defiled it."

Remember Bilhah's name means "unconcerned," as Reuben seemed to have been about the consequences of his rash and disrespectful act. However, Reuben's nonchalance may have come from another rash act he had heard about some years back, surrounding the mandrakes he had worked so hard to get for his mother.

Genesis 30:17 – So when Jacob came in from the fields that evening, Leah went out to meet him. "You must sleep with me," she said. "I have hired you with my son's mandrakes…"

Notice that Leah said, "*my son's mandrakes.*" She gave Reuben ownership of what she herself desired. If it weren't for Leah's requesting the mandrakes, it is doubtful Reuben would have ever gone searching for them. True to family history (Genesis 25:27-28), Leah created sides in the family and put Reuben squarely on hers.

While Reuben was harvesting the mandrakes, Rachel somehow found out about it. Being a person of the field, Rachel knew immediately why and for whom Reuben was looking for mandrakes and immediately how she would get them.

Genesis 30:14-15 – …Rachel said to Leah "Please give me some of your son's mandrakes." But she said to her, "Wasn't it enough that you took my husband? Will you take my son's mandrakes too?" "Very well," Rachel said, "he can sleep with you tonight in return for your son's mandrakes."

The reasons the sisters wanted the mandrakes were as different as night and day. Rachel, forever the practical one, simply wanted to increase her chances of having children, of building a family, attaining a power base. For Rachel, the mandrakes were a fertility treatment.

By the time Scripture records Reuben bringing the mandrakes to Leah, she had already given birth to four sons. Therefore, fertility was never an issue with Leah. No, Leah wanted the plants more for their narcotic and aphrodisiac effects. The one thing Leah was sure of was that it was only in bed that she could win with Jacob. Like any normal woman, Leah wanted to be wanted and desired for herself, but Leah learned long ago you don't always get what you want. The mandrakes helped in that area. The mandrakes helped both to dull her senses to this reality and fuel the ambition to take on a role—really any fantasy that would satisfy Jacob. The mandrakes took the sting out of knowing that she herself wasn't good enough.

> *Show him you care just for him,*
> *Do the things that he likes to do,*
> *Wear your hair just for him,*
> *Cause you won't get him, thinking and a praying*
> *Wishing and hoping*

> *—Wishing and Hoping–Dusty Springfield©*

With the mandrakes, Leah could pretend. Even in her desperation, Leah knew that though Jacob didn't love her, he never denied her. The mandrake's narcotic qualities allowed Leah to throw off her reserve and regrets. She could be whoever Jacob wanted her to be, even Rachel.

In a strange way, though she was Jacob's first wife, Leah was really the other woman. Perhaps when fed up with Rachel and her demanding ways, Jacob would turn to Leah. Perhaps when exhausted by having to prove himself, by wanting to prove himself to Rachel, he would go to Leah. Perhaps in moments when he realized that Rachel had the upper hand in their relationship, that he loved her more than she would ever love him, he would turn to Leah. Like a good doctor, Leah was always on call to provide sexual healing, to give Jacob the reassurance that he was all the man that *Rachel* needed him to be.

Proverbs 4:7 Wisdom is supreme; therefore get wisdom. Though it cost you all you have, get wisdom.

Remember, Rachel wasn't looking at the mandrakes as an aphrodisiac but as a fertility treatment. Like her father and like her husband, Rachel knew a weakness when she saw it. Leah couldn't see how her desperation to be in Jacob's arms was playing right into her sister's hands. Leah couldn't see how foolish it was to give Rachel the mandrakes. In giving Rachel the mandrakes, Leah afforded Rachel the means to have the one thing she had over Rachel and that was the ability to have children.

Desperate Times, Desperate Measures

Proverbs 13:16 – Every prudent man acts out of knowledge, but a fool exposes his folly.

After Rachel had the audacity to ask for the mandrakes her son had picked for her, Leah began to answer the age-old question: how low can you go, can you go down low?

As Leah fathomed the depths of self-respect, the first thing she hit was delusion. "Wasn't it enough that you took my husband?" What could Leah be questioning but her own sanity? To paraphrase God's Word concerning Esau and Jacob, Rachel he loved, Leah he slept with. She had his children, but she never had him. For Leah, Jacob was a husband in name only. There is a Hebrew word for husband – *iysh,* simply meaning "man," "male," "someone." Jacob was that someone who allowed Leah to say, "I got a man!" What happens next is the height of Leah's low point.

Genesis 30:16 – So, when Jacob came in from the fields that evening, Leah went out to meet him. "You must sleep with me," she said. "I have hired you with my son's mandrakes." So he slept with her that night.

> *What you won't do, do for love,*
> *You tried everything*
> *But you don't give up.*
> *In my world, only you*
> *Make me do for love*
> *What I would not do.*

> *–What You Won't do for Love, Bobby Caldwell©*

She went to him. He promised nothing. Her time with him was always temporary and at his convenience. He could pick her up and put her down at a moment's notice. None of this seemed to matter.

Psalm 19:13 – Keep your servant from willful sins; may they not rule over me. Then I will be blameless, innocent of great transgression.

The fact that Leah went out to meet Jacob in the evening again reveals another dimension to Leah's character that is quite different from the way she is usually portrayed. Evening was the time women usually went out to draw water or do other chores because of the cooler temperatures than those of mid-day (Genesis 24:11, John 4:7). It was not a time for a woman to go out alone just for the sake of being out. In fact, the only other woman in Scripture seen out alone in the evening without a specific purpose was the prostitute in God's Book of Wisdom called *Proverbs*.

Proverbs 7:9-10 – …at twilight, as the day was fading, as the dark of night set in. Then out came a woman to meet him, dressed like a prostitute and with crafty intent.…

Leah's intent wasn't grounded in shrewdness but insanity, which one definition states: to do the same thing and expect different results. Leah's intentions were neither good nor shrewd but stupid.

"I have hired you with my son's mandrakes." In Jesus' native language, Hebrew, the word "hired" at best means "subordinate." At worst, the word "hired" means *tanah*, "to bargain with a harlot." Leah's actions recall the words of the prophet Ezekiel.

Ezekiel 16:34 – So in your prostitution you are the opposite of others; no one runs after you for your favors. You are the very opposite, for you give payment and none is given to you.

One of the hallmarks of desperation is recklessness. And Leah readily displayed this by breaking social mores and going to Jacob at night. Some might say that for once in her life, Leah was being bold and assertive. And she was, but not because she had a God-given bold assertive spirit. Leah had simply become bolder and more assertive in her desperation.

In this sordid little scene, everybody paid a price. Rachel paid using her vulnerability (lack of children) to manipulate her sister thus continuing the strained relationship between them. Reuben paid by giving up time that could have been spent enjoying his youth. Jacob paid by showing his sons, who one day would marry and have families of their own, once more what he thought about his own. Leah, as always, paid with her favorite form of currency—self-respect. But sadly, Leah just didn't see it that way.

Genesis 30:17-19 – God listened to Leah and she became pregnant and bore Jacob a fifth son. Then Leah said, "God has rewarded me for giving my maidservant to my husband." She named him Issachar. Leah conceived again and bore Jacob a sixth son. Then Leah said, "God has presented me with a precious gift. This time my husband will treat me with honor because I have borne him six sons." So she named him Zebulun.

With the birth of six sons and the two Zilpah bore, directly and indirectly, Leah had produced three fourths of the Twelve Tribes of Israel. Yet, for all of this musical bedding, Jacob's heart remained firmly with Rachel. In fact, if anything Jacob was more in love with Rachel than ever because by this time Rachel had given birth to Joseph. What six babies couldn't get for Leah, one got for Rachel, the ultimate honor besides marriage a man can give a woman—a plan for the future.

Genesis 30:25 – After Rachel gave birth to Joseph, Jacob said to Laban, "Send me on my way so I can go back to my homeland."

It was only after Joseph was born that Jacob desired to raise his children (with Joseph in mind specifically) in his homeland—the land God promised to his fathers, the land God promised to him (Genesis 28:12).

Jacob never presented Leah with a plan. He'd never had to. With Leah, it was always "play it as it lays." For all of Jacob's legendary deception, he was consistently truthful with Leah. Years earlier he let her know he was finished with her as a husband (Genesis 29:28). Jacob never misled her. Leah did it all by herself.

Isaiah 44:20 – He feeds on ashes, a deluded heart misleads him; he cannot save himself…

In Hebrew, the word "honor" can mean *hadar* – "to favor," and *y'quar* – "dignity." In Greek the word "honor" means *time* – "to esteem." It is ironic that the Greek word is spelled like our English word "time." Time after time Leah did the very things guaranteed to produce the results she didn't want and certainly didn't need. And when they didn't work, time after time she did them again. Leah refused to see it any other way.

Ironically, Leah's insecurity grew, instead of diminishing with the birth of each of her and Zilpah's children. Rachel, on the other hand, never looked to Jacob to make her feel worthy. Unlike Leah who thanked God for giving her the opportunity to make *her* worthy in Jacob's sight, Rachel thanked God for herself and herself alone.

Genesis 30:22-23 – Then God remembered Rachel; he listened to her and opened her womb. She became pregnant and gave birth to a son and said, "God has taken away my disgrace." She named him Joseph and said, "May the Lord add to me another son."

Even with the long-awaited birth of Joseph, there isn't a reference to Jacob. Rachel thanked God for removing the stigma of being barren, a serious one for a woman during those times, but she never thanked God for making her acceptable in Jacob's sight. Rachel clearly understood the political and social benefits of having a husband and children, particularly sons. But both Rachel and Jacob knew she could make it without him.

Proverbs 31:13,17 – She selects wool and flax and works with eager hands… She sets about her work vigorously; her arms are strong for her tasks.

Remember Rachel was a shepherdess (Genesis 29: 1-4). When push came to shove, Rachel could make a way for herself with or without a man. Rachel may have loved Jacob (although there is not one reference in the whole Jacob-Leah-Rachel narrative that has her saying such). But she certainly didn't need him.

However, Leah did. Leah needed him to prove to everybody that she was just as good or better than Rachel. She needed Jacob to make her feel beautiful and desired. Leah needed him to make her happy. She needed him to do what she could never manage to do on her own and that was to feel good about herself.

In Plain Sight

1 Samuel 26:21 – Surely I have acted like a fool and have erred greatly.

But then out of nowhere, something happened that may have made Leah stop in the name of love for herself and her children and really think about her relationship with Jacob. When Jacob went to meet his brother, Esau, as he was traveling back to Canaan, Leah may have finally seen what had been right in front of her all the time.

Genesis 33:1-2 – Jacob looked up and there was Esau, coming with his four hundred men; so he divided the children among Leah, Rachel and the two maidservants. He put the maidservants and their children in front, Leah and her children next, and Rachel and Joseph in the rear.

Leah had held nothing back. She did everything she could and then some. And for all that, Jacob casually placed her smack dab in the middle of what could be trouble as he prepared to meet the brother he tricked out of his inheritance years ago (Genesis 27:1-41).

Genesis 33:5-7 – Then Esau looked up and saw the women and the children. "Who are these with you?" he asked. Jacob answered, "They are the children God has graciously given your servant." Then the maidservants and their children approached and bowed down. Next, Leah and her children came and bowed down. Last of all came Joseph and Rachel, and they too bowed down.

Out of all the children, the only one introduced by name was Joseph, his son by Rachel. Though still a child, Joseph was mentioned even before his mother, a foreshadowing of the rule he (and his sons) would one day have over the family (Genesis 48:15-20, 49:22-26).

After this incident, perhaps for the first time in her life, Leah began to come to grips with the reality of her situation. Middle: neither one extreme nor the other, just something intermediate. That's what she had been all her life. She was in between her father and Rachel, and likewise Jacob and Rachel. Jacob didn't love her but he didn't hate her either. She was just his in between.

Ecclesiastes 6:9 – Better what the eyes sees than the roving of the appetite. This too is meaningless, a chasing after the wind.

Leah had made excuses for his behavior and that of her own. But this may have been the final insult heaped on top of all the others that she couldn't excuse. She had given him six beautiful sons and he couldn't introduce her or them by name to his brother? What had she done but love him beyond reason that he should disrespect her so? Jacob had shown everybody better than he could tell them what he thought of her. At last it was quite clear to her. There was nothing else for her to say or do. After the meeting with Esau, Leah disappears from Scripture in an active sense.

> *I tried to do the best I can for you but*
> *it seems it's not enough.*
> *And you know I care, even when you're not*
> *there; but it's not what you want.*
>
> *I Tried – Angela Bofill©*

Meanwhile Rachel had been praying for another son ever since the birth of Joseph (Genesis 30:24). Never in doubt about Jacob's love, Rachel wanted more leverage, more power. But be careful what you pray for. The Lord blessed Rachel with exactly what she wanted, another son and he was the death of her.

Genesis 35:16-18 – …Rachel began to give birth and had great difficulty. And as she was having great difficulty in childbirth, the midwife said to her, "Don't be afraid for you have another son." As she breathed her last – for she was dying – she named her son Ben-Oni. But his father named him Benjamin.

Ben-Oni means "son of my pain." However, Jacob made a decision that the second child of his beloved Rachel would not have a name that carried an element of sadness, so he changed his name to Benjamin, which means "son of my right hand," symbolizing power and authority (Genesis 35:16-18).

In the whole Jacob, Leah, and Rachel narrative, this is the only time that Jacob took charge of naming one of his children, including Joseph.[35] In Biblical times, it was commonly believed that a name reflected the very essence of a person. Naming a child was very important and not to be taken lightly. Parents often named their children based on the circumstances and their emotions surrounding their children's birth. Also taken into account were the parents' hopes and dreams for their child. In addition an aspect of the worship of God was often added to a child's name *(example 'El, one of the root names for God added onto a name, i.e., Samuel).*

Jacob named Benjamin out of the emotions he had for Rachel. The blatant favoritism Jacob showed toward Joseph and then Benjamin was simply an outpouring of the love he had for Rachel. With her, everything was right and so it would be for this child, this only other child by the love of his life.

Genesis 35:20 – Over her tomb, Jacob set up a pillar and to this day, that pillar marks Rachel's tomb.

---

35 In the Old Testament, the majority of the name givers to children even in this patriarchal society, were the mothers. Also, Old Testament children were named shortly after birth, whereas by the time of the New Testament names were given eight days after birth to coincide with circumcision.

Previously, Jacob had set up pillars for the worship of God (Genesis 28:18) and as a boundary between his territory and that of Laban's (Genesis 31:44-47). Rachel was the only woman in the Bible to have a monument built in her honor.

> *I love you*
> *And you alone were meant for me*
> *Please give your loving heart to me*
> *And say we'll never part.*
> *I think of you every morning*
> *Dream of you every night*
> *Darling, I'm never lonely*
> *Whenever you are in sight*

> *–(I Love You) for Sentimental Reasons, Nat King Cole©*

Rachel took pre-eminence over Leah even in death.

Genesis 49:29-31 – Then he gave them these instructions: "I am about to be gathered to my people. Bury me with my fathers in the cave in the field of Ephron the Hittite, the cave in the field of Machpelah, near Mamre in Canaan, which Abraham bought as a burial place from Ephron the Hittite, along with the field. There Abraham and his wife, Sarah were buried, there Isaac and his wife Rebekah were buried, and there I buried Leah."

Contrast *"and there I buried Leah"* with Jacob's heartfelt talk about Rachel's death.

Genesis 48:7 – As I was returning from Paddan, to my sorrow Rachel died in the land of Canaan while we were still on the way, a little distance from Ephrath. So I buried her there beside the road to Ephrath (that is, Bethlehem).[36]

The death of Rachel did nothing to advance Leah's cause with Jacob. He didn't turn to her, not even for consolation. What must have gone through Leah's mind (as well as the children's) as she watched her husband build a monument to her sister? He had never done anything like that for her. He had never built anything for her. He had never really worked for her. She had done it all. Didn't she deserve a monument?

Isaiah 49:4 – But I said, "I have labored to no purpose; I have spent my strength in vain and for nothing. Yet what is due me is in the Lord's hand, and my reward is with my God."

The Esau incident was one thing, but the monument was another. Esau was gone but the monument was there and would be there for everyone to see how much her husband loved her *sister*. At this point, though Rachel suffered physical death before Leah. Leah's spirit probably died and simply waited for her body to catch up to it.

As Jacob comforted himself with memories of the love he had with Rachel, Leah was tormented over love that she never got, no matter how hard she tried. She had stopped having babies. What was she to do? She really didn't know anything else. And now Leah couldn't see past the regrets and self-recriminations to how much her daughter needed her.

---

36 Ephrath was the ancient name for Bethlehem. Bethlehem was located in the district of Ephrath. Ephrath means "fertility" and Bethlehem means "house of bread." It is the ancestral home of David and earthly birthplace of Jesus Christ *(Micah 5:2,Matthew 2:1, Luke 2:4, 11-15)*.

Dinah

Genesis 34:1-2 – Now Dinah, the daughter Leah had borne to Jacob, went out to visit the women of the land. When Shechem son of Hamor the Hivite, the ruler of that area, saw her, he took her and violated her.

Dinah, whose name means "one who judges," was the only girl born to Jacob and Leah. She was the seventh and the last child Leah gave birth to. Quite a few years had passed since Leah had given birth to the last of her sons, Zebulun. In naming her daughter, Scripture doesn't write of Leah saddling her like she did her sons with the burden of making her marriage work. Dinah entered the world responsible for no one's happiness but her own (Genesis 30:21).

Since most Biblical scholars pen Leah's death before the initial migration to Egypt[37] to escape the famine detailed during the Joseph narrative, Leah was still alive at this point but merely going through the motions. Jacob was old and Leah was tired. Dinah's brothers were much older and they were not around. They learned long ago by being around you see too much. Without Rachel, Jacob preferred to stay away from home as well, because how could it be one without *her* there? This was the environment Dinah spent her childhood in, a home filled with people trying to escape from it.

The Septuagint (the Greek translation of the Bible) says Dinah *"went forth to observe the daughters of the inhabitants."* [38]

---

37 *Genesis 42:1- 26* outlines Jacob's family going to Egypt. Verse 5, 7: *Then Jacob left Beersheba, and Israel's sons took their father Jacob and their children and their wives in the carts that Pharaoh had sent to transport him... He took with him to Egypt his sons and grandsons and his daughters and granddaughters – all his offspring.* Leah is only mentioned in the past tense in verse 15.

38 The inhabitants were the Hivites, descendant of Ham *(Genesis 10:6). T*hey were commonly referred to as one of the groups of nations to be removed from the Land of Canaan by the Lord *(Deuteronomy 7:1, Joshua 3:10).* The religion worshipped by the Hivites at this time was the Canaanite god Baal (or a derivative of).

It should be noted that the chief god of these inhabitants (Hivites), as for much of the Canaanite peoples, was Baal, a god worshipped with much sensuality. Was Dinah just momentarily escaping from the sadness of her home or determined to get to a place, any place, where people were living instead of simply existing?

Jacob was either home or very close by when Dinah left (Genesis 34:5). Why didn't he forbid her leaving? Or did he protest only to have Dinah ignore him? Dinah may have thought how he never had much to say to her or her brothers, especially when *Rachel* was alive. Now it was too late. It was too late for him to talk and for her to listen. How could he possibly tell her what she could and couldn't do, what was right or wrong? No, it was too late for all of that. It was too late for him to try to be her father.

Dinah may have also made a judgment call that it was already too late for her mother. And the thought may have crossed her mind that if she hung around any longer, it would be too late for her as well. She didn't want to be sad. She didn't want to be lonely. She didn't want to retreat from life like her mother, not when there was a great big world right outside her door.

> *The lights are much brighter there, you*
> *can forget all your troubles, forget all your cares*
> *and go downtown, things'll be great when you're*
> *downtown, no finer place for sure, downtown*
> *everything's waiting for you.*

–Downtown, Petula Clark©

Since her brothers were out in the fields when the rape happened (Genesis 34:5), other than Jacob the only other person at home would have had to have been Leah. So why didn't Leah try to stop her daughter from venturing out among the Hivite women? Why didn't Leah say anything? Maybe by her silence Leah gave her consent. As Dinah walked out, perhaps Leah saw herself years ago when she had ventured out one evening all for the sake of love.

Genesis 34:3-4 – His heart was drawn to Dinah daughter of Jacob, and he loved the girl and spoke tenderly to her. And Shechem said to his father Hamor, "Get me this girl as my wife."

Genesis 34:8 – But Hamor said to them, "My son Shechem has his heart set on your daughter. Please give her to him as his wife."

Genesis 34: 11-12 – Then Shechem said to Dinah's father and brothers," Let me find favor in your eyes, and I will give you whatever you ask. Make the price for the bride and the gift I am to bring as great as you like, and I'll pay whatever you ask me. Only give me the girl as my wife."

Especially in the Old Testament, fathers played the lead in arranging and negotiating marriages; although mothers would at times have a say as well (Genesis 26:34-35, 27:46). When Shechem, the rapist, fell in love with Dinah and sought to make things right by making her his wife, Leah was conspicuous by her absence.

Nothing she had ever said mattered—to her father, her sister, and certainly not Jacob. At this point, whatever she thought, she kept to herself which was easy to do since most of her family including her husband barely came around.

Her sons were grown with lives of their own. Her husband was, is, and would always be one in name only. Her sister was dead. Her daughter, her only daughter, had wanted to leave and when she did she was raped. Her daughter was more afraid of staying inside with her family than going outside to strangers. But who could blame her for wanting to escape? All Leah had now were memories more bitter than sweet.

In my solitude you haunt me
With reveries of days gone by
In my solitude you taunt me
With memories that never die
I sit in my chair and filled with despair
Nobody could be so sad
With gloom everywhere, I sit and I stare
I'll know that I'll soon go mad
in my solitude...

—Solitude, Billie Holiday©

Also, Leah couldn't help but think as wrong as it started out at least Shechem loved Dinah. He wanted her and her alone. From what Leah could see and hear, Shechem wouldn't wake up one morning disgusted that her daughter was lying beside him. Shechem wanted Dinah to be his wife to love and cherish, to have and to hold until death do them part. He was willing to do anything and pay anything for the privilege of having Dinah's hand in marriage. It didn't look like he would be "finished" with her any time soon.

Leah reasoned to herself that, yes ,Shechem "took" Dinah, but he wouldn't rob her of her self-esteem. When Shechem spoke of Dinah, Leah heard tenderness in his voice, something she had never heard in Jacob's.

Genesis 34:31 – But they replied, "Should he have treated our sister like a prostitute?"

That was what Simeon and Levi—Jacob's and Leah's second and third oldest sons—said after their killing and looting spree against Hamor and Shechem as well as every male in the city of Shechem in revenge for the rape of their sister (Genesis 34: 25-26).

When made aware of what his sons had done; Jacob voiced more concern about retaliation of the various Canaanite tribes once word of the Shechem massacre got out, than his daughter's honor and safety (Genesis 34:30-31).

However, Jacob's sons were no longer boys but men. They were men who chose not to listen to their father. Since Jacob wasn't going to act, they would. They determined to bring their sister back regardless of what their father had promised Hamor and Shechem. Their father's promises meant nothing to them. As the oldest brothers, they would be the father to their sister that Jacob failed to be for them. They would do for their sister what their father never did for their mother—honor her.

Leah's Legacy: Faded from View

Like mother like daughter?

Dinah is never mentioned again in Scripture, with the exception of a genealogical reference in (Genesis 46:15). God's Word never tells us if she ever married. We don't know if she ever found true love and happiness or tragically like her mother—lived out her days in confusion, regret, and despair.

Whenever Leah and Rachel are written about together in the Bible, Rachel's name comes first even though Leah was the oldest.

Family, friends, and associates of David's great grandfather, Boaz, said this upon his marriage to Ruth the Moabitess:

Ruth 4:11 – Then the elders and all those at the gate said, "We are witnesses. May the Lord make the woman who is coming into your home like Rachel and Leah, who together built up the Israel. May you have standing in Ephrathah and be famous in Bethlehem.

Rachel was the younger and she had far fewer children than Leah, but the elders, the wise and powerful (*...at the gate*) mentioned her name first as a better example for Ruth to follow than that of Leah because Rachel's focus was on family, inheritance, and legacy (Genesis 31:14-21).

Five women are listed in the genealogy of Jesus Christ in *Matthew 1:1-16:*

Tamar (*verse 3*)
Rahab (*verse 5*)
Ruth (*verse 5*)

Uriah's wife (*verse 6*)[39]
Mary (*verse 16*)

Tellingly, Leah, the mother of Judah, the tribe through which Jesus Christ would come, isn't.

Mark 3:33 – Who are my mother and my brothers? He asked.

Luke 8:21 – ...My mother and brothers are those who hear God's word and put it into practice.

---

39 *David was the father of Solomon, whose mother had been Uriah's wife.* This was Bathsheba.

Athaliah

THE BIG PAYBACK

Athaliah

Galatians 6:7 (KJV) – Be not deceived; God is not mocked: for whatsoever a man soweth; that shall he also reap.

Athaliah was the only woman to sit on a throne of Israel. She was the only person not of Davidic descent to sit where God promised the ancestors of David would (1 Kings 9:5). She placed her name in a place where God said He would place His. Athaliah means "Jehovah is strong."

How Athaliah came to sit where she sat is a cautionary tale for those full of ambition and anger. Her story is a warning to all who seem to have an axe to grind... all the time.

Athaliah first comes on the scene in 2 Kings 8:18—introduced as the wife of Jehoram, the fifth king of Judah—and not in a flattering way.

2 Kings 8:16-18 – In the fifth year of Joram son of Ahab king of Israel, when Jehoshaphat was king of Judah, Jehoram son of Jehoshaphat began his reign as king of Judah. He was thirty-two years old when he became king, and he reigned in Jerusalem eight years. He walked in the ways of the kings of Israel, as the house of Ahab had done, for he married a daughter of Ahab.

Family Matters

Athaliah's story, like everyone's story, begins with family. Though God's Word clearly states Ahab as Athaliah's father, it is never said outright that Jezebel is her mother. Since her name has a Hebraic meaning, Athaliah may have been a child Ahab had with another wife or concubine of Israelite descent.

Most of what we know about Athaliah comes from her father's side of the family. Ahab was the son of Omri who founded the dynasty that ruled the Northern Kingdom for approximately 40 years. It is interesting that only once is Athaliah referred to as Ahab's daughter, while 2 Kings 8:26 and 2 Chronicles 22:2 identify her as the granddaughter of Omri. Like the word "son," the word "daughter" is not only defined as just the direct female offspring of a husband and wife but any female descendant of that family or even a person of the same temperament and actions. It would be the spirit of Omri—bold, ambitious, ruthless, and shrewd— rather than that of Ahab that would manifest itself and intensify in Athaliah.

It was Omri who arranged the marriage of Athaliah's father, Ahab, to an unrepentant preacher's daughter by the name of Jezebel (daughter of Ethbaal, king/priest of Tyre and Sidon) for commercial and diplomatic considerations (1 Kings 16:31).[40]

As strong as Omri was as a leader, his son Ahab was weak as a follower, especially of Jezebel. Theirs was that suffocating kind of love that squeezed out everyone else, including their children. It must have been difficult for Athaliah growing up as a bit player in the drama of Ahab and Jezebel. It must have been hard, but it would not be without its lessons.

---

40 According to the ancient Jewish historian Josephus, quoting the Phoenician historian Menander the Ephesian: Ethbaal was a priest of Asarte/Ashtoreth. He murdered the previous king and founded a dynasty that lasted approximately 32 years (*Flavius Josephus Against Apion 1.18*).

Deuteronomy 7:3-4 – Do not intermarry with them. Do not give your daughters to their sons or take their daughters for your sons, for they will turn your sons away from following me to serve other gods...

Ahab allowed Jezebel to take the lead concerning their household as well as the affairs of the state. With Ahab's blessing, Jezebel also took the reins in promoting her religion. The goddess Ashtoreth was the patron saint of Tyre and Sidon. Followers of Ashtoreth had a heightened appreciation for the tremendous power of sex and war that she represented.

Proverbs 22:6 – Train a child in the way he should go and when he is old he will not turn from it.

Although married to the king of Israel, it would not be the God of Abraham, Isaac, and Jacob that Athaliah would learn of and worship. Throughout her life, Athaliah would adhere to what she had been taught since childhood and what she knew best: sex and violence.[41]

How did this Baal-worshiping, vulgar, and violent woman come into the family of God?

---

41 The Canaanite goddess Ashtoreth was worshipped as a consort of Baal in Tyre and Sidon. Though Ashtoreth is primarily looked upon as a goddess of sensuality (from where the Greeks would interpret her as Aphrodite), Ashtoreth was a goddess of fertility, sexuality, and war.

By Invitation Only

Do you ever wonder why some families are mired in mess (and usually the same mess) generation after generation? Do you ever wonder why some families continue to suffer from repeated bad decisions and their consequences? Do you ever wonder why some family members have managed to tear down the strongholds of their lives and strive to the next level, incorporating a "spirit of power, love, and self-discipline" (2 Timothy 1:7), while other family members work feverishly to tear down the ones tearing down the strongholds?

The answer to these vexing questions is a constant infusion of fresh recruits, full to the brim with dysfunction. They are either brought in or birthed in. Either way, they come ready to join forces with family demons already present. They are like matches in a household of leaking gas.

Athaliah was brought in. She came by invitation.

2 Chronicles 18:1 – Now Jehoshaphat had great wealth and honor and he allied himself with Ahab through marriage.

One of the major themes surrounding the Athaliah story is that history keeps tragically repeating itself. If insanity means doing the same thing and expecting different results, then one of Judah's greatest kings was a little touched. Jehoshaphat, the fourth king of Judah (after the nation of Israel split into the Northern and Southern Kingdoms), had an almost fatal attraction to the Northern Kingdom in the person of King Ahab. Despite the phenomenal blessings God bestowed on him during his reign, for whatever reason, Jehoshaphat was constantly impressed and influenced by Ahab. Throughout his life, he would play the country cousin to Ahab's city slicker.

2 Corinthians 6:14 – Do not be yoked with unbelievers. For what do righteousness and wickedness have in common…

Jehoshaphat could have looked in the not-so-distant past of his own family to know the consequences of ungodly relationships. Jehoshaphat couldn't say he didn't know. He couldn't say he hadn't been warned of the danger foreign women presented to men of God.

1 Kings 11:1, 4-5 – King Solomon loved many foreign women… As Solomon grew old, his wives turned his heart after other gods, and his heart was not fully devoted to the Lord his God, as the heart of David his father had been. He followed Ashtoreth the goddess of the Sidonians…

And now, here was Jehoshaphat giving his blessing to the marriage of his son Jehoram to a woman of Sidonian nature, despite what he knew, despite what he had seen with his very own eyes in the marriage of Ahab and Jezebel.

Isaiah 30:1 – "Woe to the obstinate children, declares the Lord, "to those who carry out plans that are not mine, forming an alliance, but not by my Spirit…"

When choosing a bride for a son, parents (with the father leading the arrangement) usually chose a bride based on her ability to fit into the family, to be a productive member of that family, and make it more prosperous by bearing children (sons).

By custom, Jehoshaphat had to pay Ahab a bride price, compensation for the lost labor and the hoped-for sons that Athaliah would bring to Jehoshaphat's family. The bride price Ahab requested of Jehoshaphat was an alliance against the Arameans and their king Ben-Hadad. Ahab saw the need for additional forces and resources to take back important trading and commercial centers like Ramoth Gilead (1 Kings 20:34, 22:2-3). Jehoshaphat had them (2 Chronicles 17:12-19). Ahab flattered Jehoshaphat and invited him to share in the profits to come from the conquest (2 Chronicles 18:1-3, 1 Kings 22:1-4).

Added to the promises of military conquest and financial prosperity, the bride price consisted of the added benefit of solving a growing problem in the Ahab household. From her Biblical biography, we know that Jezebel was loath to share Ahab's heart or the spotlight with anyone. Perhaps urged on by Jezebel to get Athaliah out of the house and out of her way, the offer of Athaliah to Jehoshaphat's son gave Ahab peace on Jezebel's terms. Jezebel would have the pleasure of saying good riddance to the only other woman mentioned in Ahab's court, and the only other rival for Ahab's affection and attention. With all this in mind, Ahab presents Jehoshaphat an offer he should have refused.

Proverbs 1:10 – My son if sinners entice you, do not give into them.

When it was time for Athaliah to leave Samaria and her father's house for Jerusalem as Jehoram's wife, she would leave with an overwhelming need for control, to be seen and heard without regard for anyone or anything. Control was something Athaliah never had in her father's house—not with Jezebel in it.

James 3:14-16 – But if you harbor bitter envy and selfish ambition in your hearts, do not boast about it or deny the truth. Such wisdom does not come down from heaven but is earthly, unspiritual, of the devil. For where you have envy and selfish ambition, there you find disorder and every evil practice.

Athaliah was uprooted from everything she had ever known. She had been taken away from her father, all because of Jezebel. Athaliah had no doubt about that. On her way to Jerusalem, Athalaiah had time to think and wonder what that kind of power felt like—power like Jezebel had. She determined to one day have it but not like Jezebel. For Athaliah, raised on the same stage but never in the spotlight, behind the scenes would never do.

Gotta find me a future move outta my way
I want it all, I want it all, I want it all and I want it now
I want it all, (yes I want it all), I want it all (hey)
I want it all and I want it now

—I Want it All, Queen©

Kindred Spirits

2 Kings 8:17-18 – He was thirty-two years old when he became king and reigned in Jerusalem eight years. He walked in the ways of the kings of Israel as the house of Ahab had done, for he married a daughter of Ahab.

Jehoram, whose name means "Jehovah is exalted," co-reigned with his father, Jehoshaphat, for five years (853-848 B.C.) and eight years on his own. Including the co-regency with his father, Jehoram reigned over the Kingdom of Judah for a total of 13 years. The number 13 traditionally is seen as unlucky and a harbinger of ill will. Speaking of Jehoram and his reign, this was quite true. Jehoram's 13 year reign, deeply influenced by Athaliah, was a period of rebellion, apostasy, and chaos.

Genesis 2:24 – For this reason a man will leave his father and mother and be united to his wife, and they will become one flesh.

The word "flesh" connotes several ideas in the Bible. It can mean the union of physical bodies as written in the above verse. But it can also mean, especially in the case of Jehoram and Athaliah, their shared lusts and desires. One of the Hebrew words for "flesh" would ominously portend how both Jehoram and Athaliah would get whatever they wanted. The word is *tibehah*, which means "butchery."

Jehoram was Athaliah's Ahab, a man easily and gladly led down the wrong path. He was the stereotypical weak son of a strong, charismatic father. However, he inherited Jehoshaphat's insecurities and took them to new levels or more accurately—depths. He masked his insecurities with grand gestures of cruelty, namely against those least suspecting of it—his family.

2 Chronicles 21:4 – When Jehoram established himself firmly over his father's kingdom, he put all his brothers to the sword along with some of the princes of Israel.

The six brothers Jehoram had killed are listed in 2 Chronicles 21:2. They were given wealth and power by their father, Jehoshaphat, though not as much as had been given to Jehoram, for as the oldest, he was given the kingdom. But apparently what Jehoshaphat gave to Jehoram's brothers was more than Jehoram and Athaliah could take.

By himself, Jehoram didn't have the guts to murder his relatives, but he was advised how to have it done by someone who did. Who could have influenced Jehoram to kill his brothers and those belonging to the House of David (2 Chronicles 21:2) but one who had been taught firsthand that rivals are never to be tolerated but always destroyed?

Ezekiel 16:47 – You not only walked in their ways and copied their detestable practices, but in all your ways you soon became more depraved than they.

Oddly though, Athaliah and Jehoram were married. Scripture never describes Athaliah as Jehoram's wife. We know the Biblical meaning of the word "wife" is a helpmate. In Hebrew the word "mate" is always female (*uwth – female associate*). But the word "help" in Hebrew has one meaning that stands out in relation to the woman we know as Athaliah and the relationship she had with her husband and the kingdom of Judah. That word is *chazaq,* which means "to fasten upon, to seize."

Jehoram proved to be that insecure, empty vessel Athaliah could seize upon and pour all her ambitions into, helping herself to the power and prestige she could not get in Samaria where she had to contend with Jezebel. However, in Jerusalem, in the city where God said he would place his name, Athaliah saw an opportunity to make one for herself.

Skilled in the arts of seduction and assassination through the worship of the Ashtoreth, Athaliah played to Jehoram's ego and she played rough. As his malevolent cheerleader, Athaliah made Jehoram feel invincible and impervious to anything anyone might want to say—including God. Athaliah reinforced for him lessons she had learned while growing up in Samaria, that in order to get things done your way, some people either had to get out or be taken out of your way. Jehoram's murder of his brothers was the culmination of all he learned, not from the God of his father but from his wife.

During this period, when Jehoram and Athaliah were running roughshod over anyone and everyone, notably Scripture does not mention the moral speed bumps such as the priests and prophets in this part of the narrative.

Drawing on the lessons of stepmother Jezebel (1 Kings 21:1-10), Athaliah may have bought them off or threatened to kill them off. Fearful and corrupt, knowing the fate of Jehoram's relatives, they remained silent and became silent partners in Jehoram and Athaliah's crimes. However, even if a priest or prophet had dared confront Jehoram and Athaliah, they would not have been listened to.

2 Timothy 4:3-4 – For the time will come when men will not put up with sound doctrine. Instead, to suit their own desires, they will gather around them a great number of teachers to say what their itching ears want to hear. They will turn their ears away from the truth and turn aside to myths.

Besides Athaliah, there were others who Jehoram relied on who counseled him. They were neither priests nor prophets of God. Instead they were friends of the family—specifically Athaliah's.

Romans 16:18 – For such people are not serving our Lord Christ, but their own appetites. By smooth talk and flattery they deceive the minds of naïve people.

Like his father, Jehoshaphat, Jehoram had a stupid streak when it came to friends and family. He naively thought that Athaliah and the advisors she brought with her were looking out for his best interest and helping him when all the while they were helping themselves.

Hebrews 3:7 – …Today, if you hear his voice, do not harden your hearts….

It's important to note that in coming to Jerusalem, Athaliah had a wonderful opportunity to hear the voice of God. However, by bringing a sizable contingent of advisors and counselors from Samaria, she made a deliberate choice not to. Athaliah had come out from under the shadow of Jezebel. She was more than a queen. As far as both she and Jehoram were concerned, Athaliah was co-regent. What on earth could this God she heard some call Jehovah Elohe Israel (The Lord God of Israel) tell her that she didn't already know?

Isaiah 43:18-19 – Forget the former things; do not dwell on the past. See, I am doing a new thing! Now it springs up; do you not perceive it?

Athaliah had come from Samaria to Jerusalem, a new city to her. But unfortunately, she came with old baggage. She could have left it behind, but by bringing along preachers, teachers, and others from home, Athaliah insured the impossibility of letting go or even changing. In Athaliah's mind, she was fine just the way she was and she made sure she brought along people who she could depend on to second that emotion.

Athaliah's old baggage—in the form of cohorts from Samaria, prevented her from leaving behind the resentments and grudges of the past. God had presented Athaliah with the opportunity of a new location and position that could have affected her disposition. Like Michal, Athaliah rejected the opportunity of charting a new course for a new life. Athaliah felt no need to change because in her mind, why change for the better when the worst is serving you so well?

Revelation 2:21 – I have given her time to repent of her immorality, but she is unwilling.

With Jehoshaphat dead along with Jehoram's brothers and other potentially meddlesome family members, Athaliah and Jehoram were free to do whatever they wished. They were a law unto themselves (Romans 2:14), and everyone including priest and prophet knew to obey. Things had never looked better.

> *These are the good times*
> *Our new state of mind*
> *These are the good times*
>
> *–Good Times, Chic©*

However, just as Jehoram and Athaliah thought they had everything and everybody under control, they forgot about the one who controls the times and seasons (Daniel 2:21). They didn't hear the forecast—stormy weather.

2 Chronicles 21:16-17 – The Lord aroused against Jehoram the hostility of the Philistines and of the Arabs who lived near the Cushites. They attacked Judah, invaded it and carried off all the goods found in the king's palace, together with his sons and wives. – Not a son was left to him except Ahaziah, the youngest.

Prior to this event, the prophet Elijah had sent Jehoram a letter condemning him for his evil ways (2 Chronicles 21:12-15). Elijah pointedly wrote to him that he had "walked in the way of the kings of Israel." The prophet told Jehoram that the consequences of his actions would be sickness and death. The result of this stinging indictment was neither remorse nor repentance on Jehoram's part but contempt.

It didn't matter to Jehoram that this was the same prophet who had stood up to Ahab (1 Kings 18:16-18, 21:17-22). Clueless and contemptuous of his family's history and faith, it didn't register with Jehoram that this was the same prophet who had humiliated his mother-in-law, Jezebel, and defeated the gods both she and his wife worshipped (1 Kings: 18:19-39).

Psalm 34:21 – Evil will slay the wicked, the foes of the righteous will be condemned.

Soon after the attacks, Jehoram was afflicted with a disease of the bowels. For two years he suffered in great pain until he died. It happened just as Elijah, the man of God Jehoram had ignored, said that it would.

2 Chronicles 21:18-19 – ...the Lord afflicted Jehoram with an incurable disease of the bowels. In the course of time, at the end of the second year, his bowels came out because of the disease, and he died in great pain. His people made no fire in his honor, as they had for his fathers.

While Jehoram was alive, the people of Jerusalem could not and would not say anything, knowing the fate of his siblings or anyone else who may have dared to say the emperor had no clothes. However when he died, the people gave vent to their true feelings. How could they give honor to the man who, though he was king, was totally ruled by someone else?

2 Chronicles 21:20 – ...He passed away to no one's regret, and was buried in the city of David, but not in the tomb of the kings.

Athaliah, being Athaliah, probably could not help but notice this affront to her husband, her family, herself. It was an act of blatant disrespect, a slap not only in her face but especially her son, Ahaziah's, as well. Althaliah took this indignity to heart. As she always did, Athaliah would remember this wrong that had been done to her. She would remember it well and sooner rather than later, the people of Jerusalem would know that where she came from there is no such thing as turning the other cheek.

Matthew 15:19 – For out of the heart come evil thoughts, murder, adultery, sexual immorality, theft, false testimony, slander.

Ahaziah – Mama's Dearest

Since God's word implies that the sons who were kidnapped in the attacks were those of his other "wives" (2 Chronicles 21:17), Ahaziah may have been the only child of Jehoram and Athaliah. It's quite interesting that both she and Ahaziah survived those attacks. During that time, Athaliah and Ahaziah may have been visiting a place Athaliah considered her true home, a place of memories both good and bad, but her home nonetheless—Samaria. Perhaps, she had taken Ahaziah to the place that had taught her so much that she wanted to make sure her son learned the same lessons.

Ahaziah was 22 when he ascended to the throne of Judah. Ahaziah, whose name means "Jehovah sustains," may have been named by Athaliah after her brother, Ahab's son and successor.[42] Ahaziah lived only one year after ascending to the throne of Judah. The primary reason for his abbreviated life was his obedience to his mother. Just as she dominated her husband, Athaliah dominated her son. Just as her advisors counseled her husband, her advisors counseled her son.

2 Chronicles 22:3 – He too walked in the ways of the house of Ahab, for his mother encouraged him in doing wrong. He did evil in the eyes of the Lord, as the house of Ahab had done, for after his father's death they became his advisers to his undoing.

Their advice to the young king was to engage in déjà vu. Mother and friends advised Ahaziah to join his uncle, the king of Israel (Athaliah's younger brother, named Joram[43]) in war against the Aramean King Hazael at Ramoth

---

42   Ahaziah succeeded Ahab and was the ninth king of Israel reigning from 853 to 852 B.C.
43   Joram, also spelled Jehoram, succeeded his brother Ahaziah as the king of Israel from 852 to 841 B.C.

Gilead. The decision to once again go to war against King Hazael was an attempt by Athaliah, the de facto ruler, to address unfinished business.

A powerful lesson here is that along with history, sin also repeats itself from generation to generation. It not only repeats itself but intensifies, upping the ante of the consequences that must be reaped. Ahab had been killed in the first battle and Jehoshaphat had almost met the same fate (1 Kings 22:29-35). But that was then, and now there was no one around to warn and even if there were, there was no one around who would take heed.

Proverbs 26:11 – As a dog returns to its vomit, so a fool repeats his folly.

Pushing Ahaziah into joining Joram in the war for Ramoth Gilead afforded Athaliah the opportunity of killing two birds with one stone. First, she could avenge the death of her father (1 Kings 22:31-38). Secondly, the war offered political pluses. Victory would solidify Ahaziah's position and thus secure Athaliah's. After all, everyone loves a war hero.

Unlike the last time, there would be no third-party meddling in the form of a priest or prophet, as the prophet Micaiah had done with Ahab. There would be no Jehoshaphat to interfere either, for it was he who had called on the prophet Micaiah in the first place to bless the venture, which he didn't (1 Kings 22:7-8).

Athaliah would show Ahaziah that they didn't need anybody to bless their plans. Their success was in their hands. Wasn't she the granddaughter of Omri who had built Samaria? Wasn't she the daughter of Ahab who had adorned it?[44] Wasn't Ahaziah her son? Ahaziah would see. This time would be different. Mother was in control.

---

44   Ahab was a developer of great skill as referenced in his obituary *1 Kings 22:39*. He oversaw projects that made Samaria, the capital of the Northern Kings, a symbol grandeur and decadence referenced in *Amos 3:15* and *6:4*.

I'm in control, never gonna stop
Control, to get what I want
Control, I like to have a lot
Control now I'm all grown up

—Control, Janet Jackson©

In Ramoth Gilead the sequel, Joram, like his father, was wounded in battle.

2 Kings 8:28-29 – Ahaziah went with Joram son of Ahab to war against Hazael *king of Aram at Ramoth Gilead. The Arameans wounded Joram… so King Joram returned to Jezreel to recover from the wounds the Arameans had inflicted on him at Ramoth in his battle with Hazael king of Aram. Then Ahaziah son of Jehoram king of Judah went down to Jezreel to see Joram son of Ahab, because he had been wounded.*

Both Athaliah and Ahaziah, along with Joram, probably thought this was but a minor setback to their plans. Without a doubt, Athaliah sent Ahaziah off to Jezreel with much pomp and circumstance and assurances of victory. Athaliah had it all planned. Ahaziah would go bolster his uncle and together they would go on to win Ramoth Gilead. This was only the beginning. She and Ahaziah would resurrect the dynasty of Omri and take it to greater heights. But little did Athaliah know, as she said goodbye to her son—her only son—it would be the last time she would see him alive.

Instead of leading victorious armies, Joram and Ahaziah would be chased and hunted down like dogs by Jehu—whose name means *"the Lord is he"*—a military commander (perhaps one of King Joram's leading officers – 2 Kings 9:1-5).

Jehu, anointed by the prophet Elisha, was the instrument the Lord chose to exact judgment against the house of Ahab (2 Kings 9:6-10). However, by continually joining in with the house of Ahab, Jehoshaphat's descendants would share in their judgment as well.

Proverbs 1:29-32 – Since they hated knowledge and did not choose to fear the Lord, since they would not accept my advice and spurned my rebuke, they will eat the fruit of their ways and be filled with the fruit of their schemes. For the waywardness of the simple will kill them...

While Joram was recuperating from his wounds, Jehu was orchestrating a coup (2 Kings 9:14) backed by his fellow officers who viewed Joram's fighting capabilities and his running back to "mother" with less than admiration.[45] As Jehu advanced upon Jezreel, he gathered additional forces. He inspired them to overthrow Joram and the de facto ruler of the Northern Kingdom: Jezebel (2 Kings 9:16-22). By the time Joram realized Jehu's intentions, it was too late. He tried to warn his nephew, but it was too late for him also.

2 Kings 9:23 – Joram turned about and fled, calling out to Ahaziah, "Treachery Ahaziah!"

The last Ahaziah saw of his uncle was of him screaming in terror to get away from Jehu and never making it. He saw the precision of Jehu's arrow enter Joram's chest and stop his heart. He saw Jehu command *his* officers to throw his uncle, the king of Israel's, body down on a field like garbage (*2 Kings 9:26*).

1 Kings 22:34-35 – But someone drew his bow at random and hit the king of Israel (Ahab) between the sections of his armor. The king told his chariot driver, "Wheel around and get me out of the fighting. I've been wounded." All day long the battle raged, and the king was propped up in his chariot facing the Arameans. The blood from his wound ran onto the floor of the chariot and that evening he died.

45 Along with Samaria, Ahab and Jezebel had a royal residence in Jezreel (*1 Kings 21:1*). It is likely that Jezebel was here monitoring events as Athaliah was doing in Jerusalem. This is the last known residence of Jezebel up until the time of her assassination (*1 Kings 9:30-33*).

Little boy lost, dazed, and confused, Ahaziah tried in vain to run from Jehu. But the Mama's boy king was no match for a trained warrior. As death at the hands of Jehu reached out for him, the last thing Ahaziah saw wasn't so much the face of Jehu and his men, but history tragically repeating itself.

2 Kings 9:27- When Ahaziah king of Judah saw what had happened, he fled up the road to Beth Haggan. Jehu chased him, shouting "Kill him too!" They wounded him in his chariot on the way up to Gur near Ibleam, but he escaped to Megiddo and died there.

A Time to Kill

So within a year of his ascension to the throne of Judah, Ahaziah was dead on the advice of his mother.

2 Kings 9:28 – His servants took him by chariot to Jerusalem and buried him with his fathers in the City of David.

Husband and now her son—dead, all the plans, everything she had worked so hard for...gone, or so it seemed. Then Athaliah looked around and saw.

2 Chronicles 22:9 – So there was no one in the house of Ahaziah powerful enough to retain the kingdom.

Following the death of Jehoshaphat, the Davidic line had been suffering decline and decimation by their own hands and from the hand of God.[46] Willful and woeful sins had weakened the House of David until the last "man" standing was Athaliah. And now she stood alone. Even her mentor-nemesis Jezebel was dead (2 Kings 9:30-37). Standing knee-deep in the ruin of her family, Athaliah took in all the death and devastation she had experienced because of this God she heard called Jehovah-jireh (the Lord Will Provide) by the people who serve him, and determined right then and there that one good turn deserves another.

2 Chronicles 22:10 – When Athaliah the mother of Ahaziah saw that her son was dead, she proceeded to destroy the whole royal family of the house of Judah.

---

46   Jehoram killed six of his brothers along with other family members when he succeeded his father Jehoshaphat as king of Judah (*2 Chronicles 21:4*). God sent judgment in the form of Philistine and Arab raiders who attacked and kidnapped more of the royal family (*2 Chronicles 21:16-17*). Jehu killed 42 relatives of Ahaziah who had not heard of Joram, Jezebel, and Ahaziah's deaths and were on their way to Samaria to visit them (*2 Kings 10:12-14*).

In Hebrew, one of the words for destroy is *yanah*, meaning "to rage, to be violent." In Greek, one of the words for destroy is *katargeo, meaning* "to render useless." According to *Webster's Dictionary,* destroy means "to put out of existence," which is what Athaliah attempted to do to the House of David.

Romans 12:19 – Do not take revenge, my friends, but leave room for God's wrath, for it is written: "It is mine to avenge; I will repay," says the Lord.

It is said that revenge is best served on a cold plate. However, Athaliah didn't want to wait and give Jehoram's remaining relatives and others in Jerusalem, who probably resented her very presence, an opportunity to hurt her more. No, she wouldn't even give them the satisfaction of mourning, giving them time to plot and plan against her. Maybe they would send her back to Samaria to get her out of the way like Jezebel did years ago. Maybe they would have her killed. No, she would not wait and see herself the brunt of further humiliation and scorn. Athaliah would take matters into her own hand.

Athaliah would avenge her family. She would call upon Ashtoreth for every bit of destructive power to do unto them as it had been done unto her. And for Athaliah, there was no time like the present. She decided to strike while the iron, or rather the knife, was hot.

Psalm 73:6-7 – Therefore pride is their necklace; they clothe themselves with violence. From their callous hearts comes iniquity, the evil conceits of their minds know no limits.

All is fair in love and war. Murdering the remaining royalty of the house of David, both adults and children, was not only an act of revenge but also political expediency. To let even one member of Jehoram's family live would leave Athaliah vulnerable to charges of the legitimacy of her right to rule. In her murderous zeal, Athaliah came close to annihilating the Davidic line through which salvation in the person of Jesus Christ would come.

And let's be clear, Athaliah did not do this by herself. As usual, when there's wrong doing to be done, you can always find help. The advisors—those she brought with her from Samaria who knew her when—were with her now. They helped her achieve what even Jezebel couldn't. They helped her complete the lessons she had learned all those years in Samaria with her father and Jezebel. They helped her carry out the advice she gave her husband when he became king.

> *Another one bites the dust*
> *Another one bites the dust*
> *And another one gone*
> *And another one gone*
> *Another one bites the dust*
> *Hey, I'm gonna get you too*
> *Another one bites the dust*
>
> *—Another One Bites the Dust, Queen©*

Proverbs 4:16-17 – For they cannot sleep 'til they do evil; they are robbed of slumber till they make someone fall. They eat the bread of wickedness and drink the wine of violence.

Not one to cry over spilled milk or blood, probably for the first time in her life, Athaliah felt secure. All obstacles had been removed. For the first time in her life, Athaliah didn't have to take a back seat to anyone. She was no longer behind the throne but on it with all power in her hands.

These are the good times.
Our new state of mind...

−*Good Times, Chic©*

Steal Away

2 Chronicles 22:11-12 – But Jehosheba, the daughter of King Jehoram, took Joash son of Ahaziah and stole him away from among the royal princes who were about to be murdered and put him and his nurse in a bedroom. Because Jehosheba, the daughter of King Jehoram and wife of the priest Jehoiada, was Ahaziah's sister, she hid the child from Athaliah so she could not kill him. He remained hidden with them in the temple of God for six years while Athaliah ruled the land.

It was not in an ordinary bedroom that Jehosheba hid the baby Joash, but more specifically a bed chamber. The KJV passage reads "*...But Jehoshaeath, the daughter of the king, took Jo'ash the son of Ahaziah and stole him from among the king's sons that were slain, and put him and his nurse in a bedchamber.*"

A chamber was a storeroom. This one could have been used for the storing of beds and/or other furnishings. Looking at the Hebrew meaning of the word chamber: *tameion* (*secret chamber, inner room, closet*), along with the Greek word: *huperoon* (above, an upper room), we see not only the courage and faith of Jehosheba but the awesome hand of God working on behalf of his people.

Psalm 27:5 (KJV) – For in the time of trouble he shall hide me in his pavilion: in the secret of his tabernacle shall he hid me; he shall set me up upon a rock.

Jehosheba, meaning "Jehovah is her oath" was a daughter of Jehoram by a woman more than likely of Israelite descent thus the Hebraic name. Ironically, this made Jehosheba Athaliah's stepdaughter. Just as Jezebel taught stepdaughter Athaliah some valuable lessons, Jehosheba would teach Athaliah one as well, one she would never forget. Jehosheba, unlike her brother Ahaziah, was nurtured in the Word of God not Baal or Ashtoreth. Unlike Ahaziah, Jehosheba grew up fearing God, not Athaliah.

Joel 2:29 – Even on my servants, both men and women, I will pour out my Spirit in those days.

In her killing spree, Athaliah primarily focused on the male heirs of David. She did not consider the women. Athaliah naturally thought with the removal of the males all opposition to her would end. She never thought about the women, especially a particular woman of God, a wife of one of the priests (Jehoiada) that she was so dismissive of.

It is quite telling that it was Jehosheba who initially took the lead in saving a son of David from certain death. She not only took Joash but also his nurse to her husband, the priest, to shelter. One Hebrew name for nurse is *aman* (to be firm, faithful, true, to trust). When Jehoiada saw the baby and the nurse, a woman who willingly decided to go with God in spite of the danger, Jehoiada, whose name means *"the Lord knows,"* knew he and his fellow priests had been silent too long. His wife's courageous act on behalf of the House of David had both chastened Jehoiada and renewed his faith in God.

Psalm 27:1 – The Lord is my light and my salvation – whom shall I fear? The Lord is the stronghold of my life – of whom shall I be afraid?

The arrival of Jehoiada on the scene (2 Chronicles 23:11) marked the first mention of a priest since the days of Jehoshaphat. It would have been impossible for Athaliah to have believed that though she was queen God was still on the throne.

Obadiah 1:3 – The pride of your heart has deceived you, you who live in the clefts of the rocks and make your home on the heights, you who say to yourself, "Who can bring me down to the ground?"

Athaliah had achieved something no other woman had ever done. Her grandfather, Omri, and her father, Ahab, would have been proud. If she were still alive, even Jezebel would have to acknowledge that the student had become the master. What need did she have of this God she had heard some call Elohim (*the Supreme God*)?

2 Thessalonians 2:11-12 – For this reason God sends them a powerful delusion so that they will believe the lie and so that all will be condemned who have not believed the truth but have delighted in wickedness.

Initially, Athaliah's natural tendency toward paranoia kept her on high alert. No doubt she had spies in the land. But as the years passed without any tangible resistance, Athaliah assumed she had everything under control.

Psalm 73:8-9 – They scoff, and speak with malice; in their arrogance they threaten oppression. Their mouths lay claim to heaven, and their tongues take possession of the earth.

Visions of grandeur also acted to dim Athaliah's normally sensitive radar. Ahaziah was dead. Now it was solely up to Athaliah, the spiritual heir of Omri, to forge ahead with rebuilding and enlarging the dynasty that he started. Athaliah was now in position to eventually claim Judah for the Northern Kingdom and unite them both under her rule. Though contemptuous of the Southern Kingdom and its capital, Jerusalem, Athaliah understood its spiritual hold on the people and she desired to use it for her own purposes.

Luke 16:8 – For the people of this world are more shrewd in dealing with their own kind than are the people of the light.

Athaliah also understood the value of the temple. Since coming to Jerusalem, she saw that the temple made the people feel good. Their security and trust was in the temple (Jeremiah 7:4). She took note of all the feasts and festivities, the pomp and circumstance. All of it fair game for her to use. Jezebel had taught her that feasts, festivals, and other religious observances provide an excellent cover for manipulation and maintaining control.[47] Just as Ahab built up the Samaria to reflect the glory of his reign, so Athaliah wanted the temple and the city of Jerusalem itself to reflect hers.

Athaliah's dismissal of the things of God as well as the people's own dismissal of God was the main reason Jehosheba and Jehoiada could keep Joash hidden in the temple for six years. The temple was the center of worship for a god she had no use and respect for. Athaliah looked upon the Temple of God as a trophy, something she had captured, something that she had won.

Isaiah 14:13-14 – You said in your heart, I will ascend to heaven; I will raise my throne above the stars of God. I will sit enthroned on the mount of the assembly on the utmost heights of the sacred mountain. I will ascend above the tops of clouds; I will make myself like the Most High.

---

47 Jezebel had a day of fasting proclaimed as cover for falsely accusing Naboth the Jezreelite of blasphemy; eventually having him stoned so that she could seize his property that Ahab coveted since it was close to his palace (*1 Kings 21:1-16*).

Son Rise

Deuteronomy 20:2-4 – When you are about to go into battle, the priest shall come forward and address the army. He shall say: Hear, O' Israel, today you are going into battle against your enemies. Do not be fainthearted or afraid; do not be terrified or give way to panic before them. For the Lord your God is the one who goes with you to fight for you against your enemies and give you victory

There is no other mention of Athaliah until Jehoiada initiated a coup to take back the throne for the House of David beginning in 2 Chronicles, chapter 23. Jehoiada, along with five other men (2 Chronicles 23:1), formed an inner circle of a movement based not on politics but on God's promise to the House of David and to their nation. As a Levite, Jehoaida had begun to do what his ancestors had done. Though they had been guilty of great sin, they faced it and fervently turned back to God (Exodus 32:25-29). As a Levite, Jehoiada was committed to doing whatever it took to reclaim the throne for the House of David. Instead of derision, Jehoiada determined it was time to instill in Athaliah fear of the Lord.

Joash's name means "Jehovah supports." In Greek, the word support is *antechomai, meaning* "to adhere to, care for.", *Webster's Dictionary* defines support as: 1) to hold in position so as to keep from falling, sinking, or slipping, 2) to keep from falling under stress, 3) to provide for, 4) to endure.

1 Kings 9:5 – I will establish your royal throne over Israel forever, as I promised David your father when I said, "You shall never fail to have a man on the throne of Israel."

All throughout the dark night of Athaliah's six-year reign, Jehoiada and those who believed God's Word, worked diligently, quietly, and prayerfully. Year in and year out, a baby was growing into a boy in the house of the Lord.

Year in and year out, Joash was being taught the faith of Abraham, Isaac, and Jacob, the history of his people and that the hope of that history rests in God alone.

Psalm 78:3-4 - …what we have heard and known, what our fathers have told us. We will not hide them from their children; we will tell the next generation the praiseworthy deeds of the Lord; his power, and the wonders he has done.

The six years Athaliah reigned symbolized both wickedness and weakness. Six stands for man's work in opposition to God. It also speaks of secular completion. Anything of man has an ending since it is the work of the created not the Creator. *1 Kings 19:18 – Yet I reserve seven thousand in Israel – all whose knees have not bowed down to Baal and all whose mouths have not kissed him.*

As the seventh year of Athaliah's rule drew near, the faith of a few had grown to inspire many. Those who refused to go along to get along, who were tired of compromise and corruption, joined Jehoiada in a cause they knew to be just (2 Chronicles 23:1-3). Seven symbolizes spiritual perfection of either good or evil. While in hiding for six years, Jehoiada had re-discovered his faith. He had been inspired by the courage of his wife. He had seen hope in the eyes of a baby destined to die. He had seen God and felt his presence. The seventh year had come. Jehoiada felt redeemed, renewed, restored, and ready. It was a perfect time to stop Athaliah.

2 Chronicles 23:1, 3-4 – In the seventh year Jehoiada showed his strength. He made a covenant with the commanders of units of a hundred…When they came to Jerusalem the whole assembly made a covenant with the king at the temple of God. Jehoiada said to them, "The king's son shall reign, as the Lord promised concerning the descendants of David."

As word spread of the return of the king; it seemed odd that Athaliah and her minions didn't notice the stirring about of priests and others who had not stirred about in years. If Athaliah did notice or hear anything different, her friends and advisors assured her not to worry. Over the years they had done everything to ensure the kingdom was firmly in her hands.

2 Chronicles 23:11-13 – Jehoiada and his sons brought out the king's son and put the crown on him; they presented him with a copy of the covenant and proclaimed him king. They anointed him and shouted, "Long live the king!" When Athaliah heard the noise of the people running and cheering the king, she went to them at the temple of the Lord. She looked, and there was the king standing by his pillar at the entrance.

The noise coming from the temple was nothing unusual, Athaliah's friends and advisors probably told her. No doubt it was one of those festivals the people were having. It was nothing for Athaliah to concern herself with. These people were always singing and shouting about something. When had all their noisy celebrations and the worship of their god ever interfered with their plans?

But something didn't feel quite right to Athaliah. She heard cheering, and to her that was unusual because she was used to and more comfortable with the silence of the people—silenced because of fear.

Out of the entire Athaliah narrative, Scripture records her speaking only once, when she saw the sole survivor of the massacre she had orchestrated seven years earlier.

2 Chronicles 23:13 – She looked and there was the king standing by his pillar at the entrance. The officers and the trumpeters were beside the king, and all the people of the land were rejoicing and blowing trumpets, and singers with musical instruments were leading the priests. Then Athaliah tore her robes and shouted "Treason! Treason!"

Years earlier, her brother Joram had cried out, "Treachery," as he was about to meet his fate (2 Kings 9:23). Now Athaliah found herself in the same predicament and just like her brother, she had no place to run.

The word "cried" in Hebrew can mean *tsa'aq* (to shriek, to proclaim) or *qara* (simply to call out). Regarding Athaliah, it most certainly didn't have the meaning of *shava* – to call for help. More than likely it was "cried" meaning *z'iq'*, to make an outcry or shout as in a battle cry. Athaliah had been at war all her life. This was her last battle. This was her last stand.

Proverbs 10:24 – What the wicked dreads will overtake him; what the righteous desire will be granted.

Since humility was never Athaliah's strong suit, in the end she defaulted to what she knew best—defiance. Seven years earlier, Athaliah had managed to pull victory from the jaws of defeat. But like a recurring nightmare, once more attention, allegiance, love, and respect were being taken away from her and given to someone else.

Isaiah 46:8-9, 11 – Remember this, fix it in mind, take it to heart, you rebels. Remember the former things, those of long ago; I am God and there is no other; I am God and there is none like me. ...what I have said, that I will bring about; what I have planned, that I will do.

"*Treason! Treason!*" Athaliah screamed the words that in essence defined her life as one of open rebellion against God.

Looking around, Athaliah's brilliant, twisted mind couldn't fathom defeat. She had surpassed Jezebel in power. She had avenged her son's death and won out over this God she heard some call Jehovah Nissi (The Lord is My Banner).

This couldn't and shouldn't be happening, not after all the work she had done, not after everything she had been through. But as the crowd around the temple grew larger and their cheers louder (2 Chronicles 23:12), the sobering reality of the end finally churned in Athaliah's stomach and came out of her mouth as an accusation against everyone and everything that had been against her, seemingly from the moment she was born. Despite her best efforts, the payback she issued seven years ago had come full circle.

"Treason! Treason!"

That shout, that war cry—who was Athaliah calling out to? Where were all the advisors she brought with her from Samaria so long ago? Where were her spies and henchman? When she needed a god, hers went into hiding in the form of Mattan, a priest of Baal Athaliah had installed in Jerusalem and whose name ironically means "gift of God.'"

Deuteronomy 7:5-6 – This is what you are to do to them: Break down their altars, smash their sacred stones, cut down their Asherah poles and burn their idols in the fire. For you are a people holy to the Lord your God.

Emboldened by Jehoiada and his men along with the sight of Joash, the people who had long lived in terror, converged on the temple of Baal and killed Mattan in front of his own altar (2 Chronicles 23:16-17). In the end, seduction and sedition failed Athaliah.

"Treason! Treason!"

2 Kings 11:15-16 – …Bring her out between the ranks and put to the sword anyone who follows her. For the priest had said, "she must not be put to death in the temple of the Lord." So they seized her as she reached the place where the horses enter the palace grounds, and there she was put to death.[48]

"Treason! Treason!"

Webster's Dictionary defines "treason" as an overt act(s) to overthrow a government. But in Hebrew, the only translation for the word "treason" is *qesher*, meaning "unlawful alliance." And this takes us right back to the beginning of the Athaliah saga. Athaliah didn't force herself into the family of God. They invited her in and not many lived to regret it.

When she needed them most; those who had followed her, whether from Samaria or from Jerusalem, who had aided and abetted her in her ambitions, were nowhere to be found. Many were probably killed during the revolt of Jehoiada, many others had scattered like vermin fleeing the light, leaving Athaliah to her own defenses.

Jeremiah 4:18 – Your own conduct and actions have brought this upon you. This is your punishment. How bitter it is! How it pierces the heart!

What's fascinating is that in and of themselves, Athaliah had many admirable qualities. She was a smart woman, an ambitious woman, a bold and decisive woman. However, her pathological issues negated them all. She refused any and all opportunities to know the great I AM. Because Athaliah lacked *"the one who is in you is greater than the one who is in the world,"* (1 John 4:4) her demons ate her alive. The worst of her got the best of her. Athaliah died defiant, despised, and alone.

---

48   Death by association: Athaliah's death echoes that of Jezebel. *2 Kings 9:33 – Throw her (Jezebel) down! Jehu said. So they threw her down, and some of her blood splattered the wall and the horses as they trampled her underfoot.* Much of the mention of horses in the Bible is metaphorical. They are used to symbolize war, power devoid of spirit. They are featured prominently in the Apocalypse in *Revelation 6:1-8.*

Matthew 26:52 – ...for all who draw the sword will die by the sword.

As her life ebbed away from the multiple stab wounds, one last thing probably crossed Athaliah's mind. She was about to be moved out of the way for good. Jezebel, the woman she hated and yet modeled herself after, lives on in the New Testament.[49] Not so for Athaliah. The last mention of Athaliah in Scripture is simply an obituary of thanks for her demise (2 Kings 11:20, 2 Chronicles 23:21). After her death, her name never appears in Scripture again.

The word "vanish" is so apt for Athaliah because of its Hebrew and Greek meaning. In Hebrew vanish means *malach,* "to disappear to dust." The Greek word for vanish is *katarego,* which means "to be rendered entirely useless," just as she tried to do to the Davidic family. However, it is *Webster's Dictionary* that provides the most telling definition regarding Athaliah's life. According to *Webster's* the word "vanish" means 1) to pass completely from existence, and 2) to assume the value of zero.

Job 3:25 – What I feared has come upon me; what I dreaded has happened to me.

Athaliah wanted so much to have control over others. She confused intimidation with respect and manipulation with love. She sat on the throne of God's Kingdom and stood for nothing and was finally reduced to such.

2 Chronicles 23:21 – ...and all the people of the land rejoiced. And the city was quiet, because Athaliah had been slain with the sword.

The word "sword" is often used in the Bible as a symbol for God's Holy Word.

---

49 The name Jezebel is used as a symbol of compromise and licentiousness creeping into the church of Thyatira (*Revelation 2:20*).

The word "quiet" in Hebrew has a number of meanings which are all related to a state of well-being (*shalev* - carefree, secure, being at ease; *shalem* - complete, friendly, safe; *shequet* - tranquility). In Greek, the word for quiet is *eirene*, meaning "peace, health, and prosperity."

Proverbs 11:10 – When the righteous prosper the city rejoices; when the wicked perish, there are shouts of joy.

After Athaliah was killed, the people she had intimidated for six years chose not to bury her.[50] As the people of Judah and Jerusalem had felt about her husband, Jehoram, when he died (2 Chronicles 21:19-20), they felt even more disgusted with even the idea of a burial for Athaliah. Even Jezebel was thought more worthy of a burial than Athaliah. It just so happened that when it came time to bury Jezebel there just wasn't enough left to bury.

2 Kings 9:34-35 – Jehu went in and ate and drank, "Take care of that cursed woman," he said, "and bury her, for she was a king's daughter." But when they went out to bury her, they found nothing except her skull, feet and hands.

In Athaliah's case, there's never a discussion.

Proverbs 26:1 – Like snow in summer or rain in harvest, honor is not fitting a fool.[51]

Athaliah's body (or that which was left of it) may have been taken out to the Valley of Hinnon—the city dump of Jerusalem.[52] It burned day and night, fed with a steady supply of all manner of waste. A putrid haze constantly

50 For a body not to be buried was considered as a sign of God's judgment and a shame for the deceased's family as well.

51 The most foolish person of all denies the reality of God: (*Psalm 14:1, 53:1*)

52 A deep narrow ravine south of Jerusalem. The Valley of Hinnon served as a kind of city dump. All matter of waste and refuse ended up there: dead animals, other remains, garbage of all forms with the putrid smell of death and decay. The Valley of Hinnon translated in Greek is *gehenna*, the word for hell.

surrounded it. The sight and smell of it made the Valley of Hinnon an apt metaphor for Hell.

In her arrogance, Athaliah had tried to reduce the Kingdom of Judah to nothing but a notch on her belt. She sought to strip it of meaning and significance other than the fact that she ruled it. In the end, she herself proved to be useless and insignificant in the Kingdom of God. And in the Kingdom of God, useless things are thrown into the fire. She who had raised so much hell now found herself on her way there.

In the end, Athaliah's name proved correct—*Jehovah is strong.*

Job 19:29 – You should fear the sword yourselves; for wrath will bring punishment by the sword, and then you will know that there is judgment.

EPILOGUE

The common thread that runs through the lives of Michal, Leah, and Athaliah is one of desperation. Their desperation caused their homicidal, obsessive, and delusional behaviors that wreaked havoc in their lives and the lives of those around them.

There are several definitions for "desperate" that each of these women exhibit to one extreme or another.

Desperate: to be both in despair and intense, as Michal was to get David back—to get back to a place and time that existed only in her mind. Michal was so desperate to relive the past she never gave herself a chance to have a future.

Desperate: an unbearable need and the anxiety surrounding the awareness of that need was Leah. Leah was desperate to love and be loved. She only got her sense of security and worth in Jacob's arms. So, she was always anxious to get back to that place as painful and humiliating as it was. Leah's desperation caused her to lose all sense of self-respect and dignity.

Desperate: reckless and violent because of despair would be Athaliah. Athaliah was desperate to be in control, mainly so she could settle old scores that reminded her of her own vulnerability. Athaliah kept pulling off the scab of old hurts, so they never healed but stayed open and raw. She then used them as justification for inflicting more harm. Athaliah constantly drew from a deep well of rage and her cup was always running over. For a while she got the power and prestige she always wanted. In the end she was stripped of both. She died alone and was quickly forgotten.

I hope these three lives have given us pause to think and reasons to act on any and everything that keeps us from being confident in the love of our

Lord and Savior Jesus Christ. If we believe his Word, what do we have to be desperate about? He is always willing and able to help us be what he created us to be, which is the very best!

Psalm 139:14 – I praise you because I am fearfully and wonderfully made; your works are wonderful. I know that full well.

ACKNOWLEDGMENTS

I would like to thank my family and friends for their support during this endeavor. I would especially like to thank my brother, Robin Dale Jones, who always believes in me and always wants the best for me. I thank my church family at Trinity United Church of Christ in Chicago, Illinois. Thanks to my pew partners at the 7:30 a.m. service. I thank my Thursday night Bible class taught by my mentor and friend, Reverend William Vance, who extols us to "keep reading." Thanks to my encourager in writing, Ms. Luesther ("The Colonel") Chapman who leads the Saturday Adult Bible Class at Trinity United Church of Christ. Much love and appreciation to the Saturday Bible School and especially "The Mighty First and Second Graders" God allowed me to work with for many years. I didn't teach them nearly as much as they taught me. They will forever be a tremendous blessing in my life.

I thank the talents and hard work of several people who were instrumental in this work: Michelle Chester, editor extraordinaire (www.ebm-services.com), the gifted graphic artist and designer, Heather UpChurch (heatherannechaney@ yahoo.com). Thank you Proof Positive Papers (www.proofpositivepapers.com).

Last but not least I thank my pastor, Reverend Otis Moss III, and my pastor Emeritus, Reverend Dr. Jeremiah A. Wright Jr., for preaching the Word of God, teaching the Word of God, and exhorting us to apply the Word of God both to our lives and the lives of all those we meet on this journey called life. Thanks to all of you for helping me grow in my faith. Thanks be to God for each and every one of you.

Works Cited

Unless otherwise noted, all Bible Scriptures are taken from the New International Version.

Bullinger, E. W. (1967) – Number in Scripture, Kregel Publications

Freeman, J (1984) – The New Manners and Customs of the Bible, Bridge-Logos Publishers

Nelson's New Illustrated Bible Dictionary (1995) – Thomas Nelson Publishers

Richards, S. L. (1999) – Every Woman in the Bible – Thomas Nelson Publishers

Strong's Complete Dictionary of Bible Words – English, Hebrew and Greek (1996) – Thomas Nelson Publishers

Whiston, W (1998) – Josephus - The Complete Works, Thomas Nelson Publishers

Lyrics to all songs used by the kind permission of Hal Leonard Corporation 2011 and Sony ATV 2011.

www.ingramcontent.com/pod-product-compliance
Lightning Source LLC
Chambersburg PA
CBHW021200020426
42331CB00003B/149